The Complete Professional Horse Racing System

The Complete Professional Horse Racing System

W. J. Davies

foulsham
LONDON • NEW YORK • TORONTO • SYDNEY

foulsham

The Publishing House, Bennetts Close,
Cippenham, Berkshire, SL1 5AP

ISBN 0-572-01713-8

Copyright © 1992 Strathearn Publishing Ltd.

Phototypeset by Typesetting Solutions, Slough, Berks.
Printed in Great Britain at St. Edmundsbury Press, Bury St. Edmunds.

CONTENTS

THE SECRET   6

1. FINDING THE RIGHT HORSES IN
   THE RIGHT RACES   9

2. THE BASICS   18

3. BETTING TAX   34

4. THE PROFIT TARGET METHOD —   56
   Three Against The Field

5. THE PROFIT TARGET METHOD —   74
   Four Against The Field

6. THE PROFIT TARGET METHOD —   84
   Five Against The Field

7. THE PROFIT TARGET METHOD —   89
   Six Against The Field

8. THE SET AMOUNT METHOD —   94
   Two Against The Field

9. THE SET AMOUNT METHOD —   111
   Three Plus Against The Field

APPENDIX — Computer Programs   131

YOUR STAKING TABLES   175

THE SECRET

Bill Davies was laying bets when most of us were at our mother's knee. Perhaps even earlier! He was a Horse Racing Man at a time when it was still very much the Sport of Kings; when professional betting men were still quite numerous. His was an era when life was that bit more gentlemanly; a time when wily old professional gamblers would pass on their secrets to aspiring young successors.

In this book Bill Davies continues this tradition. He passes on some of the most profound *"bet think"* that you can find. Like most great secrets it's simple, not complicated. You will end up *betting the odds*, not the horses! In turn this makes you more of a bookmaker than a punter and everybody knows that the bookmakers win — not the punters.

Picking winners is very hard work! To pick them consistently is almost impossible. So how did Bill Davies do it? He picked more than one. Perhaps two, three or four in the same race! That makes winning very much easier!

It's obvious when you think about it. Three horses in the same race, battling against each other to be your winner is a much more comfortable way of sitting on a bet! All you have to do is learn how to lay the bets to maximise the profit. That is Bill Davies' secret.

Here in one book is a full explanation of a proven formula for what you might have thought impossible. In many races, big races with runners at big prices in particular, you can in fact back quite a few horses against the field and make absolutely sure of a profit whichever of your selections wins. Some of the most successful professional backers in racing history have used the basic idea in the past, but never before have their methods been revealed and developed so comprehensively as in the following pages.

You can operate the Davies formula by either determining how much you wish to stake, or by setting yourself a specific profit target. For the formula to work the odds have to be right, but in races where they are, and they are not too difficult to find, formula bets improve on level stake betting.

Take a look at this series of bets on three horses in the one race at a level £10 stake:

£10 Runner A at 7-4
£10 Runner B at 5-1
£10 Runner C at 10-1

If either Runner B or Runner C wins, you show a profit on the race. Runner B at 5-1 returns £60, if successful, for a gain of £30 on a total outlay of £30; Runner C returns £110 for the same outlay of £30 and a profit of £80. But what if Runner A wins? You lose, of course, for £10 at 7-4 returns only £27.50 on your £30 bet.

Now apply the Davies formula for the £30 outlay on the same horses:

	Odds	Stake	Return	Profit
Runner A	7-4	£17.56	£48.28	£18.28
Runner B	5-1	£8.05	£48.30	£18.30
Runner C	10-1	£4.39	£48.29	£18.29
Total outlay		£30.00		

Thus you have *apportioned* your stake correctly to ensure a profit whichever horse is ultimately successful, and instead of a loss on Runner A you make a profit of £18.28. Of course, you don't gain as much when the longer-priced horses win, but on any sequence of bets, racing being what it is, the horses at the shorter prices are more likely to succeed than those at longer odds. So on a typical series of bets where you pick several horses in each race, most of the winners will be at odds in the middle range, and only an occasional winner will be a big outsider. The same is true of ante post bets where all the horses are likely to be at longer odds. Given the fact that in the long term the betting market is a reasonably accurate guide to probable results, then almost certainly more successful selections will be nearer 10-1 than 20-1, and those at 33-1 or over will be very few and far between. In practically every sequence, therefore, the inevitable tendency of shorter priced winners, means that the formula will always improve on bets at level stakes on exactly the same horses.

That in a nutshell is why the formula works. This book gives many fascinating applications of it. In its more complicated forms you may need a microcomputer to apply it, so for computer buffs, complete programs are given in each case. For most of us however, the extensive staking tables, that anyone can use, show at a glance how to stake correctly on many combinations of the most common odds.

For those who are not computer-minded or who do not own their own computer, there is the simpler *set amount* method, so all punters can operate the formula to get the best from their racing investments. Here again the handy staking tables will assist you in placing your bets.

Of course you still have to pick winners, but if you can pick out the right horses in the right races, the formula will do the rest.

It is very unusual indeed to come across something really different on the racing scene, but *The Complete Professional Horse Racing System* is just that. Nothing can guarantee a profit from backing horses, but given average luck and good judgement, the formula may help you to back more winners than ever before.

1

FINDING THE RIGHT HORSES IN THE RIGHT RACES

So staking is a vital ingredient of successful betting. But properly adjusted stakes can only do so much. If our winning formula is to function properly, obviously we have to pick out winners, and plenty of them. Also with a method that depends on backing several horses in opposition to one another, it is just as important to locate the most suitable races for this type of investment.

Small fields are clearly best avoided. Races with just a few runners produce narrow betting markets in which every animal with a realistic chance of winning is likely to be at unattractive odds. The formula cannot work effectively in such circumstances, for there will be little gain in backing a group of horses all at restricted prices.

By contrast an excellent source of sound betting opportunities for the formula can be found in the biggest races in the calendar, both on the Flat and over jumps. Here it is necesssary to distinguish between stakes races and handicaps. In the former the main adjustment in the weights to be carried are to take into account the difference of maturity between horses of different ages at different times of the year. There will also be a small sex allowance in favour of fillies and mares, and in races below the highest level there are small, automatic weight penalties for earlier successes, determined by the conditions of the particular race. In handicaps, on the other hand, the weights are deliberately framed to give every runner an equal chance. This makes the task of the punter harder, but the more generous odds on offer in such events often compensate for the extra difficulty.

The point about big races of either sort is that they are usually open affairs where the betting takes a wide range — exactly the right kind of material for the formula. From time to time there will be a 'hotpot' in a top stakes race, and the formula operator must then decide whether he intends to oppose it with bets on other animals at extended odds. But if he thinks the supposed 'good thing' may well win, he should forget the race altogether. Obviously the inclusion of an odds on favourite in a group of horses backed against the field will nearly always reduce potential profitability to the point where the possible reward is inadequate considering the risk involved. In big handicaps, however, even the market leaders are invariably at reasonable prices and there are plenty of live contenders at double-figure odds.

First, let's examine in some depth the big stakes races on the Flat. The most important of them are:

Classics for three-year-olds only
1000 Guineas Stakes (Newmarket, May)
2000 Guineas Stakes (Newmarket, May)
Derby Stakes (Epsom, June)
Oaks Stakes (Epsom, June)
St Leger Stakes (Doncaster, September)

Semi-classics for three-year-olds and over
Gold Cup (Royal Ascot, June)
Eclipse Stakes (Sandown, July)
King George VI and Queen Elizabeth Stakes (Ascot, July)
Champion Stakes (Newmarket, October)

Sprints
July Cup (Newmarket, July)
Nunthorpe Stakes (York, August)

There are plenty of other races for the best horses to contest in this country and abroad, but in terms of English racing, the above feature the absolute cream of the thoroughbreds of their generation. From the point of view of the user of the formula betting from home, they are ideal. Stable plans are well publicised via the press and a strong ante post market generally forms a few weeks before each event. It is, therefore, possible to work out bets well in advance without having to wait for betting shows only available on the morning of the race or just before the 'off', as you must do in most lesser races.

But it is no good fooling ourselves that these races are easy for the backer. The form of all the candidates will be dissected in great detail by experts in the various specialist publications. If there is an outstanding contender on form, it is bound to be at a short price. In more open events you will be hard-pressed to spot a significant form pointer that everyone else has missed.

One possible approach to the top non-handicaps on the Flat is to examine closely the form figures of the various runners. This is a fairly straightforward approach. You don't have to study collateral form lines that in theory should produce a valid comparison of the merits of the field based on weight, but which so often lead the expert up a blind alley. Just look at where a horse was placed in its last few races. If its trainer knows his job, and most certainly do, one may take it on trust that the horse has the necessary class to take its place among the best company.

It is a fact that well over half the winners of the Turf's greatest Flat races have in their record immediately before their big race triumph only a handful of the many possible combinations of two- or three- digit form figures. This trend continues season after season. The key combinations are:

11
21
131
112
122

In the case of the two-digit combinations, where a horse finished on its outing prior to the penultimate one is irrelevant. It could have been a win or a '0', or the horse may have only made just two racecourse appearances.

Armed with the knowledge of the significance of these indicators, you can go through the fancied horses, pick out those with the favoured figures, and you are at least halfway to finding the possible winner.

Are there any other factors that can be used to sort out live candidates, especially those at above average or even long prices? Well, a horse which wins a good class race by a wide margin is always worth a second look. Whilst it is true that no jockey really likes to win by farther than is necessary, competition for win and place prize money is very keen at the top. Few riders are prepared to take chances at this level and horses are nearly always ridden out to the end of the race.

Therefore go through the form of these races and look for any horse which has won by *more than three lengths* in either of its last two runs, provided this was accomplished in either a Listed or Group event. The 'pattern' which divides the most important stakes races into four categories — Listed, Group 3, Group 2 and Group 1 — is a very useful aid to winner-finding when assessing form, and, where appropriate, the relevant classification is shown in sporting dailies and other specialist publications, so qualifiers are easy enough to spot.

During the last couple of seasons alone, this idea has produced some really nice winners in the biggest races. There was the 1000 Guineas and Oaks heroine, Salsabil, even if the final starting prices of 6-4 and 2-1 were none too generous, but the Gold Cup winner that year was the 14-1 chance, Ashal which had won its warm-up Group 3 race by three and a half lengths. More recently, Mystiko (13-2, 2000 Guineas), Environment Friend (28-1, Eclipse Stakes) and Polish Patriot (6-1, July Cup) have been smashing successes for this plan from only a very limited number of qualifiers.

Turning now to big handicaps, there are of course lots of valuable events of this type run at regular intervals throughout the Flat season, but again, only a small group of really top races attract an ante post market. Unless you have inside knowledge, long-range betting months in advance runs the risk of backing animals that may not eventually run. The best time to bet is about ten days to a week before the race when the intended runners are more or less definite, as revealed by the betting lists published by the bookmakers in the sporting newspapers. Pick out your horses then. Prices usually shorten up considerably as the race approaches and employing this strategy, you could well obtain excellent value compared with the odds available on the day. On the other hand, if you do bet ante post, a non-runner is a loser, and more cautious backers may prefer to wait until the field has actually been declared to run before risking their cash.

Below is a list of the really big handicaps on which attractive early prices can be obtained:

> Lincoln Handicap (Doncaster, March)
> Chester Cup (Chester, May)
> Royal Hunt Cup (Royal Ascot, June)
> Wokingham Handicap (Royal Ascot, June)
> Northumberland Plate (Newcastle, June)
> Stewards' Cup (Goodwood, July)
> Ebor Handicap (York, August)
> Ayr Gold Cup (Ayr, September)
> Cambridgeshire Handicap (Newmarket, October)
> Cesarewitch Handicap (Newmarket, October)
> November Handicap (Doncaster, November)

Probably the best way to tackle these races and others like them is to choose a right mixture of form horses and outsiders, for of course the formula enables you to back several in each event. Prices will invariably be good enough to make this a paying game when you do find a winer.

Here are a set of recommendations which if they do not pinpoint every winner of every big handicap, will certainly point you in the right direction a lot of the time:

Form horses

Concentrate on the first eight or so horses in the betting and pay particular attention to animals that ran first or second last time out, or failing this, have recorded at least one win in their last three runs.

Outsiders

a) Look out for horses whose previous outing was in a handicap of similar importance or value, even if they ran down the field. Connections of such animals obviously fancy their chances for a big win. Things may have gone wrong in running last time, or the horse may not have 'fired' as was hoped, but it could well pop up at a long price when the betting public least expects it.

b) The favoured weight range is 8st 9lb to 8st 1lb in races of this kind where excessive weight burdens may 'anchor' good horses up against a quality field of handicappers. Therefore, examine very closely the chances of all runners, and particularly of the outsiders, actually carrying one of the nine weights from 8st 9lb down, after adjusting for any apprentice allowances. In recent years alone the Lincoln winners Amenable (22-1), K-Battery (25-1) and Cuvee Charlie (33-1), Eurolink the Lad (25-1) and Powder Blue (28-1) at Royal Ascot, Western Dancer (20-1) in the Ebor Handicap, Leysh (33-1) and Balthus (50-1) in the Cambridgeshire, and Bold Rex (20-1) in the November Handicap have all been long-priced successes off these weights, plus many more at lesser but still very remunerative odds.

c) Lightweights win their share of these events and because they do not have the class of other contenders, frequently start at big prices. The ones to look out for are those whose overall form shows evidence of the ability to win, regardless of the class of race in which they normally compete and sometimes, even if they have not performed well very recently. Two or three '1's in the six-digit form shown in all newspapers are often the tell-tale sign of a possible big win off a low weight.

National Hunt racing too has a number of races which are excellent material on which to work the formula, although with much less prize money available in the winter sport, these are far fewer than on the Flat.

The biggest non-handicaps in the jumping Calendar are the King George VI Steeple Chase at Kempton, traditionally run on Boxing Day, and the Champion Hurdle and Gold Cup, the two premier events at the Cheltenham Festival in March. Cheltenham also features a series of competitive non-handicaps of slightly less importance, all of which provide plenty of opportunities for operators of the formula.

Here the punter should avoid extreme outsiders. They do win from time to time, but on public form they are nearly always virtually impossible to spot. Stick to the first five or six in the betting on these races and you won't go far wrong. Narrowing the field down to two or three to back may not be easy, but jumpers have much longer racing careers than their Flat counterparts, and animals with proven form in the highest company are generally best. Avoid young horses just out of novice class and concentrate on form from valuable non-handicap races earlier in the season. Few animals which have made their names solely in handicaps make the grade at the very top level.

There are also a select group of big handicap steeple chases where the betting normally takes a wide range, so that a small number against the field rather than a single selection is a viable proposition with real profit potential. The Mackeson Gold Cup at Cheltenham and Newbury's Hennessey Gold Cup are two events of this sort in the first half of the season. Later on, the Grand National, Scottish National and the Whitbread Gold Cup at Sandown are the biggest ante post races where there is plenty of value in the market.

By and large, in such races you should steer clear of animals with extremely high weights. Around 11st 7lb is about the upper limit, for even very good chasers are hard put to it to hump big weights jumping fences over long distances when competing in the best handicap company. Among the lightweights, avoid horses originally handicapped at less than the minimum race weight of 10st. Details of the 'long' handicap, as it is called, are to be found in the racing press. A horse forced to carry a weight well in excess of its true handicap mark nearly always struggles against better class opponents.

In the series of valuable handicap hurdles that are run throughout the jumping year, usually on Saturdays, the 'stopping' power of weight is much less important, but both in hurdles and chases consistency and the ability to jump are the essential ingredients of success. A cursory glance at the bare form figures will indicate those animals that lack the necessary credentials, and well-backed candidates with good form do much the best. Even the Grand National at Aintree goes to a steeple chaser with proven form most years, although Ayr's Scottish equivalent can be a very difficult race. It is regularly won by a lightly weighted horse who chance 'on the book' may be far from obvious. This is very definitely a race for small stakes.

Of course you don't have to confine your use of the formula just to the big races. You can bet at prices available in betting offices in the morning or on the pre-race shows in the afternoon on any racing day, provided you have the spare time to spend.

In this respect selectivity definitely pays. Choose your races and horses with great care, and only bet when the odds seem right to ensure a decent profit.

So in the main non-handicaps are best ignored. Even in big fields the winner usually comes from the first three or four in the betting, but prices are on the whole very cramped.

Far better to concentrate on handicaps when betting at the smaller meetings. Fields with something in excess of ten runners are the safest vehicles for investment. Anything less than that and the betting market may be too narrow for the formula to produce a worthwhile gain. On the other hand, handicap races with very large numbers of moderate animals are often extremely difficult to assess and generally turn out to be a bookmaker's benefit.

As with the important handicaps, concentrate on horses that won or were second last time out, or at least have chalked up a recent win, even if they did not run too well immediately before today's race. But in run-of-the-mill handicaps horses nearer the top of the weights than the bottom are favoured, for the better animals can usually make their class tell in races where the overall standard is not high. This applies particularly 'over the sticks'. Finally, be wary of backing a horse that at some point in its career has not won over the distance of the race in which it is now competing. Most animals are very specialised in terms of their best racing distance, and if you bet on a seasoned handicapper to breaks its duck over a new distance, you are definitely bucking the percentages.

Therefore the formula, because it adjusts stakes correctly and allows you to back more than a single selection in a race, has a great deal of potential for profitable betting. On the other hand it offers no instant route to automatic riches. So don't expect to win on every race and don't bet more than you can afford to lose. But used selectively on the right horses in the right races, it does offer real prospects of a long term gain from your betting turnover.

You now have the formula with some good advice on how to apply it most advantageously. The rest is up to you!

2

THE PROFIT TARGET METHOD AND

THE BASICS

Betting to figures is the foundation of a bookmaker's business. In like manner the business of successful racing investment depends on properly adjusted staking.

At the racecourse, at the dog track or in the betting shop you will often narrow a race down to two runners which appear to have the best chances of winning. The question will then be: "which one to bet on". Back them both! The answer is to stake systematically on both selections.

As a basic example of my system, let's say you have selected two runners in a race at odds of 3-1 Runner A and 6-1 Runner B. Here's a simple and effective method of staking on both runners:

Stake for A is **B+1**
Stake for B is **A+1**.

Applying our FORMULA we have **B+1** = 6+1 = seven points on Runner A and A+1 = 3+1 = four points on Runner B. Now let our point be 50p, so our bet would be:

Runner	Odds	Bet	Stake	Return	Profit
A	3-1	50p x 7	£3.50	£14.00	£8.50
B	6-1	50p x 4	£2.00	£14.00	£8.50
			£5.50		

Total outlay £5.50. If Runner A or Runner B is the winner you recoup the total outlay and make a NET PROFIT of £8.50. It's that easy! Well with my tables it can be that easy.

Win What You Want.

You can also stake two runners so that if either runner wins you make a *particular* profit. As an example, say Runner A at 3-1 and Runner B at 6-1, profit target £5.

Runner	Odds	Stake	Return	Profit
A	3-1	£2.06	£8.24	£5.00
B	6-1	£1.18	£8.26	£5.02
		£3.24		

Total outlay £3.24. If Runner A or Runner B is the winner you recoup the total outlay and make the PROFIT TARGET of £5. There may be times when you come to believe that this is a licence to print money.

Here's the formula:

Stake for A is **B+1 x £5** divided by **A x B - 1**.
Stake for B is **A+1 x £5** divided by **A x B - 1**.

So applying the formula to odds of 3-1 and 6-1 we have:

A @ 3-1 Profit target £5.00
B @ 6-1 Profit target £5.00

Formulae: The Stake on Runner A

$$(B + 1 \times £5) \div (A \times B - 1)$$
$$(6 + 1 \times 5) \div (3 \times 6 - 1)$$
$$(7 \times 5) \div (18 - 1)$$
$$35 \div 17$$

Horse A Stake = £2.06

The Stake on Runner B

$$(A + 1 \times £5) \div (A \times B - 1)$$
$$(3 + 1 \times 5) \div (3 \times 6 - 1)$$
$$(4 \times 5) \div (18 - 1)$$
$$20 \div 17$$

Horse B Stake = £1.18

The Staking Table

Please notice that in the above example I have added 1p to adjust for the decimal places. In fact all the calculations in this book are very exact. Sometimes you may need to round them up or down to a more convenient betting unit — to make them acceptable to your bookmaker!

A good plan is to compile a TABLE of stakes in a notebook. You can then refer to it when in the betting shop. Here's how you can lay out a STAKING TABLE.

TWO AGAINST THE FIELD
(PROFIT TARGET £5)

Odds	Stake	Odds	Stake	Total Outlay
2-1	£4.01	3-1	£3.01	£7.02
2-1	£3.58	4-1	£2.15	£5.73
2-1	£3.34	5-1	£1.68	£5.02
2-1	£3.19	6-1	£1.37	£4.56
3-1	£2.28	4-1	£1.83	£4.11
3-1	£2.15	5-1	£1.44	£3.59
3-1	£2.07	6-1	£1.19	£3.26
3-1	£2.01	7-1	£1.01	£3.02
4-1	£1.59	5-1	£1.33	£2.92
4-1	£1.53	6-1	£1.10	£2.63
4-1	£1.49	7-1	£0.94	£2.43

This method of proportioning stakes can be very useful with ANTE POST bets. For example, say your ante post odds are at 15-1 and 20-1, and the profit target is £50.

Runner	Odds	Stake	Return	Profit
A	15-1	£3.52	£56.52	£50.11
B	20-1	£2.69	£56.49	£50.28
Total Outlay		£6.21		

If Runner A or Runner B wins, you recoup your outlay and make a net profit of £50.

If this is beginning to sound too easy then let me remind you that you do have to pick the right horses to get in the frame!

This is an example of a staking table for ante post bets:

TWO AGAINST THE FIELD
(Profit Target £50)

Odds	Stake	Odds	Stake	Total Outlay
10-1	£5.38	15-1	£3.70	£9.08
10-1	£5.29	20-1	£2.77	£8.06
10-1	£5.23	25-1	£2.22	£7.45
10-1	£5.19	30-1	£1.85	£7.04
15-1	£3.58	15-1	£3.58	£7.16
15-1	£3.52	20-1	£2.69	£6.21
15-1	£3.49	25-1	£2.15	£5.64
15-1	£3.46	30-1	£1.79	£5.25
16-1	£3.30	20-1	£2.67	£5.97
16-1	£3.27	25-1	£2.14	£5.41
16-1	£3.25	30-1	£1.78	£5.03
16-1	£3.23	35-1	£1.53	£4.76
20-1	£2.62	25-1	£2.11	£4.73
20-1	£2.60	30-1	£1.76	£4.36
20-1	£2.59	35-1	£1.51	£4.10

To operate the staking table you must refer to the line of the table containing your *two* odds, then read off the two stakes. For example, say odds of **15-1/20-1**. Find the 15-1/20-1 line and the stakes shown are 15-1, **£3.52** and 20-1 £2.69, total outlay £6.21. With either winner your profit will clear £50.00.

Your Betting Combinations

When taking TWO AGAINST THE FIELD we should look upon the two selections as one TEAM running on our account and the two stakes should be regarded as ONE AMOUNT sensibly divided between the two best runners in the race.

Here are staking tables for various profit targets taking two against the field.

TWO AGAINST THE FIELD
(Profit Target £2)

Odds	Stake	Odds	Stake	Total Outlay
2-1	£1.61	3-1	£1.21	£2.82
2-1	£1.44	4-1	£0.87	£2.31
2-1	£1.34	5-1	£0.68	£2.02
2-1	£1.28	6-1	£0.56	£1.84
2-1	£1.24	7-1	£0.47	£1.71
2-1	£1.21	8-1	£0.41	£1.62
2-1	£1.19	9-1	£0.36	£1.55
3-1	£0.92	4-1	£0.74	£1.66
3-1	£0.87	5-1	£0.58	£1.45
3-1	£0.83	6-1	£0.48	£1.31
3-1	£0.81	7-1	£0.41	£1.22
3-1	£0.79	8-1	£0.36	£1.15
3-1	£0.78	9-1	£0.32	£1.10
4-1	£0.64	5-1	£0.54	£1.18
4-1	£0.62	6-1	£0.44	£1.06
4-1	£0.60	7-1	£0.38	£0.98
4-1	£0.59	8-1	£0.33	£0.92
4-1	£0.58	9-1	£0.30	£0.88
4-1	£0.57	10-1	£0.27	£0.84
5-1	£0.49	6-1	£0.42	£0.91
5-1	£0.48	7-1	£0.36	£0.84
5-1	£0.47	8-1	£0.32	£0.79

TWO AGAINST THE FIELD
(Profit Target £2)

Odds	Stake	Odds	Stake	Total Outlay
5-1	£0.46	9-1	£0.28	£0.74
5-1	£0.46	10-1	£0.25	£0.71
6-1	£0.40	7-1	£0.35	£0.75
6-1	£0.39	8-1	£0.31	£0.72
6-1	£0.39	9-1	£0.27	£0.66

TWO AGAINST THE FIELD
(Profit Target £5)

Odds	Stake	Odds	Stake	Total Outlay
2-1	£4.01	3-1	£3.01	£7.02
2-1	£3.58	4-1	£2.15	£5.73
2-1	£3.34	5-1	£1.68	£5.02
2-1	£3.19	6-1	£1.37	£4.56
2-1	£3.09	7-1	£1.16	£4.25
2-1	£3.01	8-1	£1.01	£4.02
2-1	£2.95	9-1	£0.89	£3.84
3-1	£2.28	4-1	£1.83	£4.11
3-1	£2.15	5-1	£1.44	£3.59
3-1	£2.07	6-1	£1.19	£3.26
3-1	£2.01	7-1	£1.01	£3.02
4-1	£1.59	5-1	£1.33	£2.92
4-1	£1.53	6-1	£1.10	£2.63
4-1	£1.49	7-1	£0.94	£2.43
4-1	£1.46	8-1	£0.82	£2.28
4-1	£1.44	9-1	£0.72	£2.16
4-1	£1.42	10-1	£0.65	£2.07
5-1	£1.22	6-1	£1.04	£2.26
5-1	£1.19	7-1	£0.89	£2.08
5-1	£1.16	8-1	£0.78	£1.94
5-1	£1.15	9-1	£0.69	£1.84

TWO AGAINST THE FIELD
(Profit Target £5)

Odds	Stake	Odds	Stake	Total Outlay
6-1	£0.99	7-1	£0.86	£1.85
6-1	£0.97	8-1	£0.75	£1.72
6-1	£0.95	9-1	£0.67	£1.62
6-1	£0.94	10-1	£0.60	£1.54

TWO AGAINST THE FIELD
(Profit Target £8)

Odds	Stake	Odds	Stake	Total Outlay
2-1	£6.41	3-1	£4.81	£11.22
2-1	£5.72	4-1	£3.44	£9.16
2-1	£5.34	5-1	£2.68	£8.02
2-1	£5.10	6-1	£2.19	£7.29
2-1	£4.93	7-1	£1.86	£6.79
2-1	£4.81	8-1	£1.61	£6.42
2-1	£4.72	9-1	£1.42	£6.14
3-1	£3.65	4-1	£2.92	£6.57
3-1	£3.44	5-1	£2.30	£5.74
3-1	£3.30	6-1	£1.89	£5.19
3-1	£3.21	7-1	£1.61	£4.82
3-1	£3.14	8-1	£1.40	£4.54
3-1	£3.09	9-1	£1.24	£4.33
3-1	£3.04	10-1	£1.11	£4.15
4-1	£2.54	5-1	£2.12	£4.66
4-1	£2.44	6-1	£1.75	£4.19
4-1	£2.38	7-1	£1.49	£3.87
4-1	£2.33	8-1	£1.30	£3.63
4-1	£2.30	9-1	£1.15	£3.45
4-1	£2.27	10-1	£1.04	£3.31

TWO AGAINST THE FIELD
(Profit Target £8)

Odds	Stake	Odds	Stake	Total Outlay
5-1	£1.94	6-1	£1.67	£3.61
5-1	£1.89	7-1	£1.42	£3.31
5-1	£1.86	8-1	£1.24	£3.10
5-1	£1.83	9-1	£1.10	£2.93
5-1	£1.81	10-1	£0.99	£2.80
6-1	£1.57	7-1	£1.38	£2.95
6-1	£1.54	8-1	£1.20	£2.74
6-1	£1.52	9-1	£1.07	£2.59
6-1	£1.50	10-1	£0.96	£2.46

TWO AGAINST THE FIELD
(Profit Target £10)

Odds	Stake	Odds	Stake	Total Outlay
2-1	£8.01	3-1	£6.01	£14.02
2-1	£7.15	4-1	£4.30	£11.45
2-1	£6.68	5-1	£3.34	£10.02
2-1	£6.37	6-1	£2.74	£9.11
2-1	£6.16	7-1	£2.32	£8.48
2-1	£6.01	8-1	£2.01	£8.02
2-1	£5.89	9-1	£1.77	£7.66
2-1	£5.80	10-1	£1.59	£7.39
3-1	£4.56	4-1	£3.65	£8.21
3-1	£4.30	5-1	£2.87	£7.17
3-1	£4.13	6-1	£2.36	£6.49
3-1	£4.01	7-1	£2.01	£6.02
3-1	£3.92	8-1	£1.75	£5.67
3-1	£3.86	9-1	£1.55	£5.41
3-1	£3.80	10-1	£1.39	£5.19

TWO AGAINST THE FIELD
(Profit Target £10)

Odds	Stake	Odds	Stake	Total Outlay
4-1	£3.17	5-1	£2.64	£5.81
4-1	£3.05	6-1	£2.18	£5.23
4-1	£2.97	7-1	£1.86	£4.83
4-1	£2.91	8-1	£1.62	£4.53
4-1	£2.87	9-1	£1.44	£4.31
4-1	£2.83	10-1	£1.29	£4.12
5-1	£2.42	6-1	£2.08	£4.50
5-1	£2.36	7-1	£1.77	£4.13
5-1	£2.32	8-1	£1.55	£3.87
5-1	£2.28	9-1	£1.37	£3.65
5-1	£2.25	10-1	£1.23	£3.48

Now Let's Beef It Up A Little

Astute punters move on to operate the DOUBLE PROFIT method of staking.

Let's take odds of Runner A 10-1 and Runner B 15-1. Here's the bet at 50p per point.

Runner	Odds	Stake	Return	Profit
A	10-1	£3.10	£34.10	£29.80
B	15-1	£1.20	£19.20	£14.90
		£4.30		

Total outlay £4.30. Runner A doubles the net profit of Runner B. If Runner A wins, net profit = £29.80. If Runner B wins, net profit = £14.90.

Here is the formula:

Stake for A is 2 x **B** + 1.
Stake for B is **A** + 2.

Let's apply our formula with odds of A **3-1** and B **6-1**.

Stake for A is (2 x **6**) + 1 = 13 (at 50p) = £6.50.
Stake for B is (**3** + 2) = 5 (at 50p) = £2.50.
Total Stake = £9.00

3-1 × £6.50 returns £26 = Profit £17.
6-1 × £2.50 returns £17.05 = Profit £8.50

Total outlay £9, net profit A £17, B £8.50.

Win Only Half As Much When You Lose!

Stakes can also be apportioned so that a *specified* profit target from your favoured selection will be twice that of the danger selection.

For example, say Runner A at **9-4** and Runner B at **9-2**, profit targets £6 and £3.

Runner	Odds	Stake	Return	Profit
A	**9-4**	£3.29	£10.69	£6.00
B	**9-2**	£1.40	£7.70	£3.01
		£4.69		

Runner A doubles the net profit of Runner B. Total outlay £4.69. If Runner A wins net profit is £6. If Runner B wins net profit is £3.

Here is the formula:

Stake for A = Profit 1 x B + P2 divided by A x B - 1.
Stake for B = Profit 2 x A + P1 divided by A x B - 1.

So if we apply the formula for odds of 3-1 and 6-1 we have:

THE EXAMPLE BET

A @ 3-1   Profit target £6.00 = P1
B @ 6-1   Profit target £3.00 = P2

ELEMENTS OF THE FORMULA

P2 = Double profit from Runner A
P1 = Single profit from Runner B

FORMULAE

The stake on Runner A

$$([B \times P1] + P2) \div (A \times B - 1)$$
$$([6 \times 6] + 3) \div (3 \times 6 - 1)$$
$$(\quad 36 \quad + 3) \div (\quad 18 \quad - 1)$$
$$39 \quad \div \quad 17$$

Horse Stake A = £2.29

The stake on Runner B

$$([A \times P2] + P1) \div (A \times B - 1)$$
$$([3 \times 3] + 6) \div (3 \times 6 - 1)$$
$$(\quad 9 \quad + 6) \div (\quad 18 \quad - 1)$$
$$15 \quad \div \quad 17$$

Horse Stake B = £0.88

Runner	Odds	Stake	Return	Profit
A	3-1	£2.29	£9.16	£5.99
B	6-1	£0.88	£6.16	£2.99
		£3.17		

Some basic Staking Tables follow, which you will need to extend.

TWO AGAINST THE FIELD

(Profit Target A £6)
(Profit Target B £3)

Odds	Stake	Odds	Stake	Total Outlay
2-1	£4.21	3-1	£2.41	£6.62
2-1	£3.87	4-1	£1.72	£5.59
2-1	£3.68	5-1	£1.34	£5.02
2-1	£3.56	6-1	£1.10	£4.66
2-1	£3.47	7-1	£0.93	£4.40
3-1	£2.46	4-1	£1.37	£3.83
3-1	£2.37	5-1	£1.08	£3.45
3-1	£2.30	6-1	£0.89	£3.19
3-1	£2.26	7-1	£0.76	£3.02
4-1	£1.75	5-1	£0.96	£2.71
4-1	£1.71	6-1	£0.79	£2.50
4-1	£1.68	7-1	£0.68	£2.36
4-1	£1.66	8-1	£0.59	£2.25
4-1	£1.64	9-1	£0.52	£2.16
5-1	£1.35	6-1	£0.73	£2.08
5-1	£1.33	7-1	£0.63	£1.96
5-1	£1.32	8-1	£0.55	£1.87
5-1	£1.31	9-1	£0.49	£1.80
5-1	£1.30	10-1	£0.44	£1.74
6-1	£1.11	7-1	£0.60	£1.71
6-1	£1.10	8-1	£0.52	£1.62
6-1	£1.09	9-1	£0.46	£1.55
6-1	£1.08	10-1	£0.42	£1.50
7-1	£0.94	8-1	£0.50	£1.44
7-1	£0.93	9-1	£0.45	£1.38
7-1	£0.92	10-1	£0.40	£1.32

TWO AGAINST THE FIELD
(Profit Target A £10) (Profit Target B £5)

Odds	Stake	Odds	Stake	Total Outlay
2-1	£7.01	3-1	£4.01	£11.02
2-1	£6.44	4-1	£2.87	£9.31
2-1	£6.12	5-1	£2.23	£8.35
2-1	£5.92	6-1	£1.83	£7.75
2-1	£5.78	7-1	£1.55	£7.33
2-1	£5.68	8-1	£1.34	£7.02
3-1	£4.10	4-1	£2.28	£6.38
3-1	£3.94	5-1	£1.80	£5.74
3-1	£3.83	6-1	£1.48	£5.31
3-1	£3.76	7-1	£1.26	£5.02
3-1	£3.71	8-1	£1.10	£4.81
3-1	£3.66	9-1	£0.97	£4.63
3-1	£3.63	10-1	£0.87	£4.50
4-1	£2.90	5-1	£1.59	£4.49
4-1	£2.84	6-1	£1.31	£4.15
4-1	£2.79	7-1	£1.12	£3.91
4-1	£2.75	8-1	£0.98	£3.73
4-1	£2.72	9-1	£0.87	£3.59
4-1	£2.70	10-1	£0.78	£3.48
5-1	£2.25	6-1	£1.22	£3.47
5-1	£2.22	7-1	£1.04	£3.26
5-1	£2.19	8-1	£0.91	£3.10
5-1	£2.17	9-1	£0.81	£2.98
5-1	£2.15	10-1	£0.72	£2.87
6-1	£1.84	7-1	£0.99	£2.83
6-1	£1.82	8-1	£0.86	£2.68
6-1	£1.80	9-1	£0.76	£2.56
6-1	£1.79	10-1	£0.69	£2.48
7-1	£1.56	8-1	£0.83	£2.39
7-1	£1.54	9-1	£0.74	£2.28
7-1	£1.53	10-1	£0.66	£2.19

TWO AGAINST THE FIELD

(Profit Target A £50)
(Profit Target B £25)

Odds	Stake	Odds	Stake	Total Outlay
10-1	£5.21	15-1	£2.02	£7.23
10-1	£5.16	20-1	£1.52	£6.68
10-1	£5.13	25-1	£1.21	£6.34
10-1	£5.11	30-1	£1.01	£6.12
10-1	£5.10	35-1	£0.87	£5.97
12-1	£4.34	15-1	£1.97	£6.31
12-1	£4.30	20-1	£1.47	£5.77
12-1	£4.27	25-1	£1.18	£5.45
12-1	£4.26	30-1	£0.98	£5.24
12-1	£4.25	35-1	£0.85	£5.10
15-1	£3.44	20-1	£1.43	£4.87
15-1	£3.42	25-1	£1.15	£4.57
15-1	£3.41	30-1	£0.96	£4.37
15-1	£3.40	35-1	£0.82	£4.22
16-1	£3.22	20-1	£1.42	£4.64
16-1	£3.21	25-1	£1.14	£4.35
16-1	£3.19	30-1	£0.95	£4.14
16-1	£3.19	35-1	£0.82	£4.01
20-1	£2.57	25-1	£1.11	£3.68
20-1	£2.56	30-1	£0.93	£3.49
20-1	£2.55	35-1	£0.80	£3.35
22-1	£2.33	25-1	£1.10	£3.43
22-1	£2.32	30-1	£0.92	£3.24
22-1	£2.32	35-1	£0.79	£3.11

TWO AGAINST THE FIELD

(Profit Target A £100)
(Profit Target B £50)

Odds	Stake	Odds	Stake	Total Outlay
10-1	£10.41	15-1	£4.04	£14.45
10-1	£10.31	20-1	£3.03	£13.34
10-1	£10.25	25-1	£2.42	£12.67
10-1	£10.21	30-1	£2.02	£12.23
12-1	£8.67	15-1	£3.92	£12.59
12-1	£8.59	20-1	£2.94	£11.53
12-1	£8.54	25-1	£2.35	£10.89
12-1	£8.51	30-1	£1.96	£10.47
15-1	£6.87	20-1	£2.85	£9.72
15-1	£6.83	25-1	£2.28	£9.11
15-1	£6.80	30-1	£1.90	£8.70
15-1	£6.78	35-1	£1.63	£8.41
16-1	£6.44	20-1	£2.83	£9.27
16-1	£6.40	25-1	£2.27	£8.67
16-1	£6.38	30-1	£1.89	£8.27
16-1	£6.36	35-1	£1.62	£7.98
20-1	£5.12	25-1	£2.21	£7.33
20-1	£5.10	30-1	£1.85	£6.95
20-1	£5.09	35-1	£1.58	£6.67
22-1	£4.65	25-1	£2.20	£6.85
22-1	£4.64	30-1	£1.83	£6.47
22-1	£4.63	35-1	£1.57	£6.20
25-1	£4.08	30-1	£1.81	£5.89
25-1	£4.07	35-1	£1.55	£5.62

And Then There Were Three

We can now take the first step in adjusting our basic formula to cover three runners in the same race. Here is the basic formula:

Stake for A is again (**B**+1).
Stake for B is again (**A**+1).
Stake for C is (**A**×**B**−1)

Try the formula with the odds of A = 3-1, B = 6-1, C = 2-1.

THE FORMULAE

$$\text{Stake for runner A} = (B + 1) = 7 \text{ points}$$
$$\text{Stake for runner B} = (A + 1) = 4 \text{ points}$$
$$\text{Stake for runner C} = (A \times B - 1)$$
$$= (3 \times 6 - 1)$$
$$= 17 \text{ points}$$

At 50p per point,. we then have **A** at £3.50, **B** at £2.00 and **C** at £8.50.

Runner	Odds	Stake	Return	Profit
A	3-1	£3.50	£14.00	Recoup
B	6-1	£2.00	£14.00	Recoup
C	2-1	£8.50	£25.50	£11.50
		£14.00		

Total outlay £14.00. If either Runners A or B manage to beat your preferred choice or main bet, then you will save your entire stake. If your first choice beats off the danger you will clear £11.50.

So already, even in its most basic form, the formula enables you to regulate your stakes to achieve specific objectives.

3

THE PROFIT TARGET
METHOD AND
BETTING TAX

On a successful bet the return is obviously higher than the stake, so the backer should pay tax on stakes rather than allow the bookmaker to deduct it from winnings. This is even more the case if the backer is confident of having more winning bets than losing ones. Readers of this book for instance!

You can incorporate *'tax paid on'* stakes into the profit target method by allowing for it in the formula.

Study the following example with two runners at odds of **A** 3-1 and **B** 6-1 with a profit target of £5.

THE EXAMPLE BET

           Runner **A** @ 3-1   Profit Target £5.00

           Runner **B** @ 6-1   Profit Target £5.00

ELEMENTS OF THE FORMULA

Odds of Runner (A) (3-1)	= **A**
Odds of Runner (B) (6-1)	= **B**
Profit on Runner (A) (£5)	= P1
Profit on Runner (B) (£5)	= P2
Tax (@10% or .10)	= T
Stake on Runner (A)	= S3
Stake on Runner (B)	= S5

FORMULAE

Stake On Runner   (A) $= S1 \div S2$

$$S1 = (P1 \times B - T) + (P2 \times 1 + T)$$
$$= (£5 \times 6 - \cdot 10) + (£5 \times 1 \cdot 10)$$
$$= (29 \cdot 9 + 5 \cdot 5)$$
$$= 35 \cdot 4$$

$$S2 = (A-T) \times (B-T) - (1 \cdot 10 \times 1 \cdot 10)$$
$$= (3 - \cdot 10) \times (6 - \cdot 10) - (1 \cdot 10 \times 1 \cdot 10)$$
$$= (2 \cdot 9 \times 5 \cdot 90) - (1 \cdot 21)$$
$$= (17 \cdot 11) - (1 \cdot 21)$$
$$= 15 \cdot 9$$

Stake On Runner (A) $= S3 = S1 \div S2$
$$= 35 \cdot 4 \div 15 \cdot 9$$
$$= £2 \cdot 23$$

Stake On Runner   (B) $= S4 \div S2$

$$S4 = (P2 \times A-T) + (P1 \times 1 + T)$$
$$= (£5 \times 3 - \cdot 10) + (£5 \times 1 \cdot 10)$$
$$= (14 \cdot 90 + 5 \cdot 50)$$
$$S4 = £20 \cdot 40$$

Stake on Runner (B) $= S5 = S4 \div S2$
$$= 20 \cdot 4 \div 15 \cdot 9$$
$$= £1 \cdot 28$$

Runner	Odds	Stake	Return	Profit
A	3-1	£2.23	£8.92	£5.06
B	6-1	£1.28	£8.96	£5.10
	Total Stake	£3.51		
	Tax (@10%)	£0.35		
	Total outlay	£3.86		

You have built into this formula a provision to include the *Tax On* the stake and secure for yourself the £5 profit target. On small bets of this kind you may feel that the formula isn't worth the aggravation for tax of only 35p. I have included it because you ought to have it available when you start laying bigger bets. And also because you ought to try to understand the basics, even if you do intend only to use the Staking tables! For the same sort of reasons I want you to look at the last of the Two Against — Profit Target Formulae. This approach is designed to allow you to manipulate the Target Profit levels. In this instance **A** is required to produce twice the amount of **B**. The odds are again **A** 3-1 and **B** 6-1 and their respective Profit Targets are **A** £6, **B** £3.

THE EXAMPLE BET

Runner A. Odds 3-1	Profit Target £6.00
Runner B. Odds 6-1	Profit Target £3.00

ELEMENTS OF THE FORMULA

Runner A Profit Target (£6)	= P1
Runner B Profit Target (£3)	= P2
Runner A Odds (3-1)	= O1
Runner B Odds (6-1)	= O2
Runner A Stake	= S3
Runner B Stake	= S6
Tax on Bet (@10% or .10)	= T

FORMULAE

The Stake on Runner A = $S1 \div S2$

$$S1 = (P1 \times [O2 - T]) + (P2 \times [1+T])$$
$$= (6 \times [6 - .10]) + (3 \times [1+.10])$$
$$= (6 \times 5.9) + (3 \times 1.10)$$
$$= 35.4 + 3.3$$
$$= 38.7$$

$$S2 = ([O1 - T] \times [O2 - T]) - (1.21)$$
$$= ([3 - .10] \times [6 - .10) - (1.21)$$
$$= (2.9 \times 5.9) - (1.21)$$
$$= 15.9$$

$$S3 = S1 \div S2$$
$$= 38.7 \div 15.9$$

The Stake on Horse A = £2.43

The Stake on Runner B = S4 ÷ S5

$$S4 = (P2 \times [O1 - T]) + (P1 \times [1 + .10])$$
$$= (3 \times [3 - .10]) + (6 \times 1.10)$$
$$= (3 \times 2.9) + (6.6)$$
$$= 8.7 + 6.6$$
$$= 15.3$$

$$S5 = ([O2 - T] \times [O1 - T]) - (1.21)$$
$$= ([6 - .10] \times [3 - .10]) - (1.21)$$
$$= (5.9 \times 2.9) - (1.21)$$
$$= 15.9$$

$$S6 = S4 \div S5$$
$$= 15.3 \div 15.9$$

The Stake on Horse B = .96

Runner	Odds	Stake	Return	Profit
A	3-1	£2.43	£9.72	£6.00
B	6-1	£0.96	£6.72	£3.00
	Total Stake	£3.39		
	Tax (@10%)	£0.33		
	Total outlay	£3.72		

If you wanted the profit target for A to be *four* times that of B then you would simply change the number values of P1 and P2 to reflect this and your staking would automatically adjust itself.

Here are some more examples of the profit target method but for wagers at ante post odds, where they begin to look much more interesting.

TWO AGAINST THE FIELD
(Ante Post Odds)
(Profit Target £20)

Runner	Odds	Stake	Return	Profit
A	10-1	£2.20	£24.20	£20.12
B	15-1	£1.51	£24.16	£20.08
	Stakes	£3.71		
	Tax	£0.37		
	Total outlay	£4.08		

Total outlay £4.08. Winner A or B recoups total outlay, net profit £20.

TWO AGAINST THE FIELD
(Ante Post Odds)
(Profit Target A £20)
(Profit Target B £10)

Runner	Odds	Stake	Return	Profit
A	10-1	£2.12	£23.32	£20.06
B	15-1	£0.84	£13.44	£10.18
	Stakes	£2.96		
	Tax	£0.30		
	Total outlay	£3.26		

Total outlay £3.26. Recoup stakes also recoup tax paid on. If Runner A wins profit is £20. If Runner B wins profit is £10.

Now here are the staking tables, inclusive of tax, for various applications of the profit target method betting on two horses against the field; including some suitable for ante post bets in which the big prices available for fancied runners can produce a very high return.

TWO AGAINST THE FIELD
(Profit Target £2)

Odds	Stake	Odds	Stake	Tax	Total
2-1	£1.87	3-1	£1.41	£0.33	£3.61
2-1	£1.62	4-1	£0.98	£0.26	£2.86
2-1	£1.49	5-1	£0.75	£0.22	£2.46
2-1	£1.41	6-1	£0.61	£0.20	£2.22
2-1	£1.35	7-1	£0.51	£0.19	£2.05
2-1	£1.31	8-1	£0.44	£0.18	£1.93
3-1	£1.00	4-1	£0.80	£0.18	£1.98
3-1	£0.93	5-1	£0.63	£0.16	£1.72
3-1	£0.89	6-1	£0.51	£0.14	£1.54
3-1	£0.86	7-1	£0.44	£0.13	£1.43
3-1	£0.84	8-1	£0.38	£0.12	£1.34
4-1	£0.68	5-1	£0.57	£0.13	£1.38
4-1	£0.65	6-1	£0.47	£0.11	£1.23
4-1	£0.63	7-1	£0.40	£0.10	£1.13
4-1	£0.62	8-1	£0.35	£0.10	£1.07
5-1	£0.52	6-1	£0.44	£0.10	£1.06
5-1	£0.50	7-1	£0.38	£0.09	£0.97
5-1	£0.49	8-1	£0.33	£0.08	£0.90
6-1	£0.42	7-1	£0.36	£0.08	£0.86
6-1	£0.41	8-1	£0.32	£0.07	£0.80

TWO AGAINST THE FIELD
(Profit Target £5)

Odds	Stake	Odds	Stake	Tax	Total
2-1	£4.66	3-1	£3.50	£0.82	£8.98
2-1	£4.04	4-1	£2.43	£0.65	£7.12
2-1	£3.71	5-1	£1.86	£0.56	£6.13
2-1	£3.51	6-1	£1.51	£0.50	£5.52
2-1	£3.37	7-1	£1.27	£0.46	£5.10
2-1	£3.27	8-1	£1.10	£0.44	£4.81
2-1	£3.19	9-1	£0.97	£0.42	£4.58
2-1	£3.14	10-1	£0.86	£0.40	£4.40
3-1	£2.49	4-1	£1.99	£0.45	£4.93
3-1	£2.32	5-1	£1.55	£0.39	£4.26
3-1	£2.21	6-1	£1.27	£0.35	£3.83
3-1	£2.14	7-1	£1.07	£0.32	£3.53
3-1	£2.08	8-1	£0.93	£0.30	£3.31
3-1	£2.04	9-1	£0.82	£0.29	£3.15
3-1	£2.01	10-1	£0.74	£0.28	£3.03
4-1	£1.69	5-1	£1.41	£0.31	£3.41
4-1	£1.62	6-1	£1.16	£0.28	£3.06
4-1	£.157	7-1	£0.98	£0.26	£2.81
4-1	£1.53	8-1	£0.85	£0.24	·£2.62
4-1	£1.50	9-1	£0.76	£0.23	£2.49
4-1	£1.48	10-1	£0.68	£0.22	£2.38
5-1	£1.27	6-1	£1.09	£0.24	£2.60
5-1	£1.24	7-1	£0.93	£0.22	£2.39
5-1	£1.21	8-1	£0.81	£0.20	£2.22
5-1	£1.19	9-1	£0.72	£0.19	£2.10
5-1	£1.17	10-1	£0.64	£0.18	£1.99
6-1	£1.02	7-1	£0.90	£0.19	£2.11
6-1	£1.00	8-1	£0.78	£0.18	£1.96
6-1	£0.98	9-1	£0.69	£0.17	£1.84
6-1	£0.97	10-1	£0.62	£0.16	£1.75

TWO AGAINST THE FIELD
(Profit Target £8)

Odds	Stake	Odds	Stake	Tax	Total
2-1	£7.45	3-1	£5.59	£1.30	£14.34
2-1	£6.46	4-1	£3.88	£1.03	£11.37
2-1	£5.94	5-1	£2.97	£0.89	£9.80
2-1	£5.61	6-1	£2.41	£0.80	£8.82
2-1	£5.39	7-1	£2.03	£0.74	£8.16
2-1	£5.23	8-1	£1.75	£0.70	£7.68
2-1	£5.11	9-1	£1.54	£0.67	£7.32
2-1	£5.01	10-1	£1.37	£0.64	£7.02
3-1	£3.97	4-1	£3.18	£0.72	£7.87
3-1	£3.70	5-1	£2.47	£0.62	£6.79
3-1	£3.53	6-1	£2.02	£0.56	£6.11
3-1	£3.41	7-1	£1.71	£0.51	£5.63
3-1	£3.33	8-1	£1.48	£0.48	£5.29
3-1	£3.26	9-1	£1.31	£0.46	£5.03
3-1	£3.21	10-1	£1.17	£0.44	£4.82
4-1	£2.69	5-1	£2.24	£0.49	£5.42
4-1	£2.58	6-1	£1.84	£0.44	£4.86
4-1	£2.50	7-1	£1.57	£0.41	£4.48
4-1	£2.44	8-1	£1.36	£0.38	£4.18
4-1	£2.40	9-1	£1.20	£0.36	£3.96
4-1	£2.36	10-1	£1.08	£0.34	£3.78
5-1	£2.03	6-1	£1.74	£0.38	£4.15
5-1	£1.97	7-1	£1.48	£0.35	£3.80
5-1	£1.93	8-1	£1.29	£0.32	£3.54
5-1	£1.90	9-1	£1.14	£0.30	£3.34
5-1	£1.87	10-1	£1.02	£0.29	£3.18
6-1	£1.63	7-1	£1.43	£0.31	£3.37
6-1	£1.60	8-1	£1.24	£0.28	£3.12
6-1	£1.57	9-1	£1.10	£0.27	£2.94
6-1	£1.55	10-1	£0.99	£0.25	£2.79

TWO AGAINST THE FIELD
(Profit Target £10)

Odds	Stake	Odds	Stake	Tax	Total
2-1	£9.31	3-1	£6.99	£1.63	£17.93
2-1	£8.07	4-1	£4.85	£1.29	£14.21
2-1	£7.42	5-1	£3.71	£1.11	£12.24
2-1	£7.01	6-1	£3.01	£1.00	£11.02
2-1	£6.73	7-1	£2.53	£0.93	£10.19
2-1	£6.53	8-1	£2.18	£0.87	£9.58
2-1	£6.38	9-1	£1.92	£0.83	£9.13
2-1	£6.26	10-1	£1.71	£0.80	£8.77
3-1	£4.96	4-1	£3.97	£0.89	£9.82
3-1	£4.63	5-1	£3.09	£0.77	£8.49
3-1	£4.41	6-1	£2.53	£0.69	£7.63
3-1	£4.27	7-1	£2.14	£0.64	£7.05
3-1	£4.16	8-1	£1.85	£0.60	£6.61
3-1	£4.08	9-1	£1.64	£0.57	£6.29
3-1	£4.01	10-1	£1.46	£0.55	£6.02
4-1	£3.36	5-1	£2.80	£0.62	£6.78
4-1	£3.22	6-1	£2.30	£0.55	£6.07
4-1	£3.12	7-1	£1.96	£0.51	£5.59
4-1	£3.05	8-1	£1.70	£0.48	£5.23
4-1	£3.00	9-1	£1.50	£0.45	£4.95
4-1	£2.95	10-1	£1.35	£0.43	£4.73
5-1	£2.54	6-1	£2.18	£0.47	£5.19
5-1	£2.46	7-1	£1.85	£0.43	£4.74
5-1	£2.41	8-1	£1.61	£0.40	£4.42
5-1	£2.37	9-1	£1.43	£0.38	£4.18
5-1	£2.34	10-1	£1.28	£0.36	£3.98
6-1	£2.04	7-1	£1.78	£0.38	£4.20
6-1	£1.99	8-1	£1.55	£0.35	£3.89
6-1	£1.96	9-1	£1.37	£0.33	£3.66
6-1	£1.93	10-1	£1.23	£0.32	£3.48

TWO AGAINST THE FIELD
(Profit Target A £5)
(Profit Target B £2)

Odds	Stake	Odds	Stake	Tax	Total
2-1	£3.89	3-1	£2.17	£0.61	£6.67
2-1	£3.51	4-1	£1.51	£0.50	£5.52
2-1	£3.31	5-1	£1.16	£0.45	£4.92
2-1	£3.18	6-1	£0.94	£0.41	£4.53
2-1	£3.09	7-1	£0.79	£0.39	£4.27
2-1	£3.03	8-1	£0.68	£0.37	£4.08
2-1	£2.98	9-1	£0.60	£0.36	£3.94
2-1	£2.95	10-1	£0.54	£0.35	£3.84
3-1	£2.16	4-1	£1.13	£0.33	£3.62
3-1	£2.06	5-1	£0.88	£0.29	£3.23
3-1	£2.00	6-1	£0.72	£0.27	£2.99
3-1	£1.96	7-1	£0.61	£0.26	£2.83
3-1	£1.93	8-1	£0.53	£0.25	£2.71
3-1	£1.91	9-1	£0.47	£0.24	£2.62
3-1	£1.89	10-1	£0.42	£0.23	£2.54
4-1	£1.50	5-1	£0.75	£0.23	£2.48
4-1	£1.46	6-1	£0.62	£0.21	£2.29
4-1	£1.44	7-1	£0.53	£0.20	£2.17
4-1	£1.42	8-1	£0.46	£0.19	£2.07
4-1	£1.40	9-1	£0.41	£0.18	£1.99
4-1	£1.39	10-1	£0.37	£0.18	£1.94
5-1	£1.15	6-1	£0.56	£0.17	£1.88
5-1	£1.14	7-1	£0.48	£0.16	£1.78
5-1	£1.12	8-1	£0.42	£0.15	£1.69
5-1	£1.11	9-1	£0.37	£0.15	£1.63
5-1	£1.10	10-1	£0.33	£0.14	£1.57
6-1	£0.94	7-1	£0.45	£0.14	£1.53
6-1	£0.93	8-1	£0.39	£0.13	£1.45
6-1	£0.92	9-1	£0.35	£0.13	£1.40
6-1	£0.91	10-1	£0.31	£0.12	£1.34

TWO AGAINST THE FIELD
(Profit Target A £8) (Profit Target B £4)

Odds	Stake	Odds	Stake	Tax	Total
2-1	£6.68	3-1	£4.27	£1.10	£12.05
2-1	£5.75	4-1	£2.66	£0.84	£9.25
2-1	£5.39	5-1	£2.03	£0.74	£8.16
2-1	£5.17	6-1	£1.65	£0.68	£7.50
2-1	£5.02	7-1	£1.39	£0.64	£7.05
2-1	£4.91	8-1	£1.20	£0.61	£6.72
2-1	£4.83	9-1	£1.05	£0.59	£6.47
2-1	£4.76	10-1	£0.94	£0.57	£6.27
3-1	£3.64	4-1	£2.32	£0.60	£6.56
3-1	£3.36	5-1	£1.58	£0.49	£5.43
3-1	£3.26	6-1	£1.29	£0.45	£5.00
3-1	£3.18	7-1	£1.10	£0.43	£4.71
3-1	£3.13	8-1	£0.95	£0.41	£4.49
3-1	£3.08	9-1	£0.84	£0.39	£4.31
3-1	£3.05	10-1	£0.75	£0.38	£4.18
4-1	£2.51	5-1	£1.59	£0.41	£4.51
4-1	£2.38	6-1	£1.13	£0.35	£3.86
4-1	£2.33	7-1	£0.96	£0.33	£3.62
4-1	£2.29	8-1	£0.83	£0.31	£3.43
4-1	£2.27	9-1	£0.74	£0.30	£3.31
4-1	£2.25	10-1	£0.66	£0.29	£3.20
5-1	£1.91	6-1	£1.21	£0.31	£3.43
5-1	£1.84	7-1	£0.88	£0.27	£2.99
5-1	£1.81	8-1	£0.77	£0.26	£2.84
5-1	£1.79	9-1	£0.68	£0.25	£2.72
5-1	£1.78	10-1	£0.61	£0.24	£2.63
6-1	£1.55	7-1	£0.98	£0.25	£2.78
6-1	£1.50	8-1	£0.72	£0.22	£2.44
6-1	£1.48	9-1	£0.64	£0.21	£2.33
6-1	£1.47	10-1	£0.58	£0.21	£2.26

TWO AGAINST THE FIELD
(Profit Target A £10)
(Profit Target B £5)

Odds	Stake	Odds	Stake	Tax	Total
3-1	£4.42	4-1	£2.53	£0.70	£7.65
3-1	£4.20	5-1	£1.97	£0.62	£6.79
3-1	£4.07	6-1	£1.61	£0.57	£6.25
3-1	£3.97	7-1	£1.37	£0.53	£5.87
3-1	£3.90	8-1	£1.19	£0.51	£5.60
3-1	£3.85	9-1	£1.05	£0.49	£5.39
3-1	£3.81	10-1	£0.94	£0.48	£5.23
4-1	£3.05	5-1	£1.71	£0.48	£5.24
4-1	£2.97	6-1	£1.41	£0.44	£4.82
4-1	£2.91	7-1	£1.20	£0.41	£4.52
4-1	£2.86	8-1	£1.04	£0.39	£4.29
4-1	£2.83	9-1	£0.92	£0.38	£4.13
4-1	£2.80	10-1	£0.83	£0.36	£3.99
5-1	£2.34	6-1	£1.29	£0.36	£3.99
5-1	£2.30	7-1	£1.10	£0.34	£3.74
5-1	£2.26	8-1	£0.96	£0.32	£3.54
5-1	£2.24	9-1	£0.85	£0.31	£3.40
5-1	£2.22	10-1	£0.76	£0.30	£3.28
6-1	£1.90	7-1	£1.04	£0.29	£3.23
6-1	£1.87	8-1	£0.90	£0.28	£3.05
6-1	£1.85	9-1	£0.80	£0.26	£2.91
6-1	£1.84	10-1	£0.72	£0.26	£2.82
7-1	£1.60	8-1	£0.86	£0.25	£2.71
7-1	£1.58	9-1	£0.77	£0.23	£2.58
7-1	£1.57	10-1	£0.69	£0.23	£2.49

TWO AGAINST THE FIELD
(Ante Post Odds)
(Profit Target £10)

Odds	Stake	Odds	Stake	Tax	Total
8-1	£1.44	10-1	£1.18	£0.26	£2.88
8-1	£1.38	15-1	£0.78	£0.22	£2.38
8-1	£1.36	20-1	£0.59	£0.20	£2.15
8-1	£1.34	25-1	£0.47	£0.18	£1.99
8-1	£1.33	30-1	£0.39	£0.17	£1.89
12-1	£0.95	10-1	£1.12	£0.21	£2.28
12-1	£0.92	15-1	£0.75	£0.17	£1.84
12-1	£0.90	20-1	£0.56	£0.15	£1.61
12-1	£0.89	25-1	£0.45	£0.13	£1.47
12-1	£0.88	30-1	£0.38	£0.13	£1.39
10-1	£1.10	15-1	£0.76	£0.19	£2.05
10-1	£1.08	20-1	£0.57	£0.17	£1.82
10-1	£1.07	25-1	£0.46	£0.15	£1.68
10-1	£1.06	30-1	£0.38	£0.14	£1.58
16-1	£0.69	15-1	£0.73	£0.14	£1.56
16-1	£0.68	20-1	£0.55	£0.12	£1.35
16-1	£0.67	25-1	£0.44	£0.11	£1.22
16-1	£0.66	30-1	£0.37	£0.10	£1.13
15-1	£0.72	20-1	£0.55	£0.13	£1.40
15-1	£0.71	25-1	£0.44	£0.12	£1.27
15-1	£0.71	30-1	£0.37	£0.11	£1.19

TWO AGAINST THE FIELD
(Ante Post Odds)   (Profit Target £15)

Odds	Stake	Odds	Stake	Tax	Total
8-1	£2.15	10-1	£1.76	£0.39	£4.30
8-1	£2.07	15-1	£1.17	£0.32	£3.56
8-1	£2.03	20-1	£0.88	£0.29	£3.20
8-1	£2.00	25-1	£0.70	£0.27	£2.97
8-1	£1.99	30-1	£0.58	£0.26	£2.83
12-1	£1.43	10-1	£1.68	£0.31	£3.42
12-1	£1.37	15-1	£1.12	£0.25	£2.74
12-1	£1.35	20-1	£0.84	£0.22	£2.41
12-1	£1.33	25-1	£0.67	£0.20	£2.20
12-1	£1.32	30-1	£0.56	£0.19	£2.07
10-1	£1.65	15-1	£1.14	£0.28	£3.07
10-1	£1.62	20-1	£0.85	£0.25	£2.72
10-1	£1.60	25-1	£0.68	£0.23	£2.51
10-1	£1.59	30-1	£0.57	£0.22	£2.38
15-1	£1.08	20-1	£0.82	£0.19	£2.09
15-1	£1.06	25-1	£0.66	£0.17	£1.89
15-1	£1.06	30-1	£0.55	£0.16	£1.77
22-1	£0.73	20-1	£0.80	£0.15	£1.68
22-1	£0.73	25-1	£0.64	£0.14	£1.51
22-1	£0.72	30-1	£0.54	£0.13	£1.39

TWO AGAINST THE FIELD
(Ante Post Odds)   (Profit Target £20)

Odds	Stake	Odds	Stake	Tax	Total
8-1	£2.87	10-1	£2.35	£0.52	£5.74
8-1	£2.76	15-1	£1.56	£0.43	£4.75
8-1	£2.70	20-1	£1.16	£0.39	£4.25
8-1	£2.67	25-1	£0.93	£0.36	£3.96
8-1	£2.65	30-1	£0.78	£0.34	£3.77

TWO AGAINST THE FIELD
(Ante Post Odds)
(Profit Target £20)

Odds	Stake	Odds	Stake	Tax	Total
10-1	£2.28	10-1	£2.28	£0.46	£5.02
10-1	£2.20	15-1	£1.51	£0.37	£4.08
10-1	£2.16	20-1	£1.13	£0.33	£3.62
10-1	£2.13	25-1	£0.91	£0.30	£3.34
10-1	£2.11	30-1	£0.76	£0.29	£3.16
12-1	£1.90	10-1	£2.24	£0.41	£4.55
12-1	£1.83	15-1	£1.49	£0.33	£3.65
12-1	£1.79	20-1	£1.11	£0.29	£3.19
12-1	£1.77	25-1	£0.89	£0.27	£2.93
12-1	£1.76	30-1	£0.74	£0.25	£2.75
15-1	£1.46	15-1	£1.46	£0.29	£3.21
15-1	£1.43	20-1	£1.09	£0.25	£2.77
15-1	£1.42	25-1	£0.88	£0.23	£2.53
15-1	£1.41	30-1	£0.73	£0.21	£2.35
16-1	£1.42	10-1	£2.19	£0.36	£3.97
16-1	£1.37	15-1	£1.45	£0.28	£3.10
16-1	£1.34	20-1	£1.09	£0.24	£2.67
16-1	£1.33	25-1	£0.87	£0.22	£2.42
16-1	£1.32	30-1	£0.73	£0.21	£2.26
20-1	£1.07	20-1	£1.07	£0.21	£2.35
20-1	£1.06	25-1	£0.86	£0.19	£2.11
20-1	£1.05	30-1	£0.72	£0.18	£1.95
22-1	£0.98	20-1	£1.07	£0.21	£2.26
22-1	£0.97	25-1	£0.86	£0.18	£2.01
22-1	£0.96	30-1	£0.71	£0.17	£1.84
25-1	£0.85	25-1	£0.85	£0.17	£1.87
25-1	£0.84	30-1	£0.71	£0.16	£1.71

TWO AGAINST THE FIELD
(Ante Post Odds)
(Profit Target £30)

Odds	Stake	Odds	Stake	Tax	Total
8-1	£4.30	10-1	£3.52	£0.78	£8.60
8-1	£4.13	15-1	£2.33	£0.65	£7.11
8-1	£4.05	20-1	£1.74	£0.58	£6.37
8-1	£4.00	25-1	£1.39	£0.54	£5.93
8-1	£3.97	30-1	£1.16	£0.51	£5.64
10-1	£3.42	10-1	£3.42	£0.68	£7.52
10-1	£3.29	15-1	£2.27	£0.56	£6.12
10-1	£3.23	20-1	£1.70	£0.49	£5.42
10-1	£3.19	25-1	£1.36	£0.46	£5.01
10-1	£3.16	30-1	£1.13	£0.43	£4.72
12-1	£2.84	10-1	£3.35	£0.62	£6.81
12-1	£2.74	15-1	£2.22	£0.50	£5.46
12-1	£2.68	20-1	£1.67	£0.44	£4.79
12-1	£2.65	25-1	£1.33	£0.40	£4.38
12-1	£2.63	30-1	£1.11	£0.37	£4.11
15-1	£2.18	15-1	£2.18	£0.44	£4.80
15-1	£2.14	20-1	£1.64	£0.38	£4.16
15-1	£2.12	25-1	£1.31	£0.34	£3.77
15-1	£2.10	30-1	£1.09	£0.32	£3.51
16-1	£2.05	15-1	£2.17	£0.42	£4.64
16-1	£2.01	20-1	£1.63	£0.36	£4.00
16-1	£1.99	25-1	£1.30	£0.33	£3.62
16-1	£1.97	30-1	£1.09	£0.31	£3.37
20-1	£1.61	20-1	£1.61	£0.32	£3.54
20-1	£1.59	25-1	£1.28	£0.29	£3.16
20-1	£1.58	30-1	£1.07	£0.27	£2.92
22-1	£1.46	20-1	£1.60	£0.31	£3.37
22-1	£1.44	25-1	£1.28	£0.27	£2.99
22-1	£1.43	30-1	£1.07	£0.25	£2.75

TWO AGAINST THE FIELD
(Ante Post Odds)   (Profit Target £30)

25-1	£1.27	25-1	£1.27	£0.25	£2.79
25-1	£1.26	30-1	£1.06	£0.23	£2.55

TWO AGAINST THE FIELD
(Ante Post Odds)   (Profit Target £50)

Odds	Stake	Odds	Stake	Tax	Total
10-1	£5.48	15-1	£3.77	£0.93	£10.18
10-1	£5.37	20-1	£2.82	£0.82	£9.01
10-1	£5.31	25-1	£2.25	£0.76	£8.32
10-1	£5.27	30-1	£1.88	£0.72	£7.87
12-1	£4.55	15-1	£3.70	£0.83	£9.08
12-1	£4.47	20-1	£2.77	£0.72	£7.96
12-1	£4.42	25-1	£2.21	£0.66	£7.29
12-1	£4.38	30-1	£1.84	£0.62	£6.84
16-1	£3.40	15-1	£3.62	£0.70	£7.72
16-1	£3.34	20-1	£2.71	£0.61	£6.66
16-1	£3.30	25-1	£2.16	£0.55	£6.01
16-1	£3.28	30-1	£1.80	£0.51	£5.59
15-1	£3.63	15-1	£3.63	£0.73	£7.99
15-1	£3.57	20-1	£2.72	£0.63	£6.92
15-1	£3.53	25-1	£2.17	£0.57	£6.27
15-1	£3.50	30-1	£1.81	£0.53	£5.84
22-1	£2.43	20-1	£2.66	£0.51	£5.60
22-1	£2.40	25-1	£2.12	£0.45	£4.97
22-1	£2.38	30-1	£1.77	£0.42	£4.57
20-1	£2.67	20-1	£2.67	£0.53	£5.87
20-1	£2.64	25-1	£2.13	£0.48	£5.25
20-1	£2.62	30-1	£1.78	£0.44	£4.84

TWO AGAINST THE FIELD
(Ante Post Odds)
(Profit Target £100)

Odds	Stake	Odds	Stake	Tax	Total
10-1	£10.95	15-1	£7.53	£1.85	£20.33
10-1	£10.74	20-1	£5.63	£1.64	£18.01
10-1	£10.61	25-1	£4.49	£1.51	£16.61
10-1	£10.53	30-1	£3.74	£1.43	£15.70
15-1	£7.26	15-1	£7.26	£1.45	£15.97
15-1	£7.12	20-1	£5.43	£1.26	£13.81
15-1	£7.04	25-1	£4.34	£1.14	£12.52
15-1	£6.99	30-1	£3.61	£1.06	£11.66
16-1	£6.67	20-1	£5.40	£1.21	£13.28
16-1	£6.60	25-1	£4.32	£1.09	£12.01
16-1	£6.55	30-1	£3.59	£1.01	£11.15
16-1	£6.51	35-1	£3.08	£0.96	£10.55
22-1	£4.84	20-1	£5.30	£1.01	£11.15
22-1	£4.79	25-1	£4.24	£0.90	£9.93
22-1	£4.75	30-1	£3.53	£0.83	£9.11
22-1	£4.73	35-1	£3.02	£0.78	£8.53
20-1	£5.33	20-1	£5.33	£1.07	£11.73
20-1	£5.27	25-1	£4.26	£0.95	£10.48
20-1	£5.23	30-1	£3.55	£0.88	£9.66

TWO AGAINST THE FIELD
(Ante Post Odds)
(Profit Target A £20)   (Profit Target B £10)

Odds	Stake	Odds	Stake	Tax	Total
10-1	£2.12	15-1	£0.84	£0.30	£3.26
10-1	£2.10	20-1	£0.63	£0.27	£3.00
10-1	£2.09	25-1	£0.50	£0.26	£2.85
10-1	£2.08	30-1	£0.42	£0.25	£2.75

TWO AGAINST THE FIELD
(Ante Post Odds)
(Profit Target A £20) (Profit Target B £10)

Odds	Stake	Odds	Stake	Tax	Total
12-1	£1.76	15-1	£0.81	£0.26	£2.83
12-1	£1.75	20-1	£0.61	£0.24	£2.60
12-1	£1.73	25-1	£0.49	£0.22	£2.44
12-1	£1.73	30-1	£0.41	£0.21	£2.35
16-1	£1.32	15-1	£0.78	£0.21	£2.31
16-1	£1.31	20-1	£0.58	£0.19	£2.08
16-1	£1.30	25-1	£0.47	£0.18	£1.95
16-1	£1.29	30-1	£0.39	£0.17	£1.85
15-1	£1.41	15-1	£0.78	£0.22	£2.41
15-1	£1.40	20-1	£0.59	£0.20	£2.19
15-1	£1.39	25-1	£0.47	£0.19	£2.05
15-1	£1.38	30-1	£0.39	£0.18	£1.95
20-1	£1.05	20-1	£0.57	£0.16	£1.78
20-1	£1.04	25-1	£0.46	£0.15	£1.65
20-1	£1.04	30-1	£0.38	£0.14	£1.56
25-1	£0.83	25-1	£0.45	£0.13	£1.41
25-1	£0.83	30-1	£0.37	£0.12	£1.32
25-1	£0.83	35-1	£0.32	£0.12	£1.27

TWO AGAINST THE FIELD
(Ante Post Odds)
(Profit Target A £40) (Profit Target B £20)

Odds	Stake	Odds	Stake	Tax	Total
8-1	£5.44	10-1	£2.63	£0.81	£8.88
8-1	£5.31	15-1	£1.74	£0.71	£7.76
8-1	£5.25	20-1	£1.30	£0.66	£7.21

TWO AGAINST THE FIELD
(Ante Post Odds)
(Profit Target A £40)   (Profit Target B £20)

Odds	Stake	Odds	Stake	Tax	Total
10-1	£4.23	15-1	£1.66	£0.59	£6.48
10-1	£4.19	20-1	£1.25	£0.54	£5.98
10-1	£4.16	25-1	£1.00	£0.52	£5.68
10-1	£4.14	30-1	£0.83	£0.50	£5.47
12-1	£3.52	15-1	£1.61	£0.51	£5.64
12-1	£3.48	20-1	£1.21	£0.47	£5.16
12-1	£3.46	25-1	£0.97	£0.44	£4.87
12-1	£3.44	30-1	£0.81	£0.43	£4.68
15-1	£2.81	15-1	£1.56	£0.44	£4.81
15-1	£2.78	20-1	£1.17	£0.39	£4.34
15-1	£2.76	25-1	£0.93	£0.37	£4.06
15-1	£2.75	30-1	£0.78	£0.35	£3.88
20-1	£2.08	20-1	£1.13	£0.32	£3.53
20-1	£2.07	25-1	£0.90	£0.30	£3.27
20-1	£2.06	30-1	£0.75	£0.28	£3.09

TWO AGAINST THE FIELD
(Ante Post Odds)
(Profit Target A £50)   (Profit Target B £25)

Odds	Stake	Odds	Stake	Tax	Total
10-1	£5.29	15-1	£2.08	£0.74	£8.11
10-1	£5.23	20-1	£1.55	£0.68	£7.46
10-1	£5.20	25-1	£1.24	£0.64	£7.08
10-1	£5.17	30-1	£1.04	£0.62	£6.83
12-1	£4.40	15-1	£2.01	£0.64	£7.05
12-1	£4.35	20-1	£1.51	£0.59	£6.45
12-1	£4.32	25-1	£1.20	£0.55	£6.07
12-1	£4.30	30-1	£1.00	£0.53	£5.83

TWO AGAINST THE FIELD
(Ante Post Odds)
(Profit Target A £50)   (Profit Target B £25)

Odds	Stake	Odds	Stake	Tax	Total
15-1	£3.51	15-1	£1.95	£0.55	£6.01
15-1	£3.47	20-1	£1.46	£0.49	£5.42
15-1	£3.45	25-1	£1.17	£0.46	£5.08
15-1	£3.44	30-1	£0.97	£0.44	£4.85
20-1	£2.60	20-1	£1.41	£0.40	£4.41
20-1	£2.58	25-1	£1.13	£0.37	£4.08
20-1	£2.57	30-1	£0.94	£0.35	£3.86
25-1	£2.07	25-1	£1.10	£0.32	£3.49
25-1	£2.06	30-1	£0.92	£0.30	£3.28

TWO AGAINST THE FIELD
(Ante Post Odds)
(Profit Target A £100)   (Profit Target B £50)

Odds	Stake	Odds	Stake	Tax	Total
10-1	£10.57	15-1	£4.15	£1.47	£16.19
10-1	£10.45	20-1	£3.10	£1.36	£14.91
10-1	£10.39	25-1	£2.48	£1.29	£14.16
10-1	£10.34	30-1	£2.06	£1.24	£13.64
12-1	£8.78	15-1	£4.01	£1.28	£14.07
12-1	£8.69	20-1	£3.00	£1.17	£12.86
12-1	£8.63	25-1	£2.40	£1.10	£12.13
12-1	£8.60	30-1	£2.00	£1.06	£11.66
15-1	£7.01	15-1	£3.88	£1.09	£11.98
15-1	£6.94	20-1	£2.91	£0.98	£10.83
15-1	£6.89	25-1	£2.32	£0.92	£10.13
15-1	£6.86	30-1	£1.93	£0.88	£9.67

TWO AGAINST THE FIELD
(Ante Post Odds)
(Profit Target A £100)   (Profit Target B £50)

Odds	Stake	Odds	Stake	Tax	Total
20-1	£5.19	20-1	£2.81	£0.80	£8.80
20-1	£5.16	25-1	£2.25	£0.74	£8.15
20-1	£5.14	30-1	£1.87	£0.70	£7.71
25-1	£4.12	25-1	£2.20	£0.63	£6.95
25-1	£4.11	30-1	£1.83	£0.59	£6.53
25-1	£4.10	35-1	£1.57	£0.57	£6.24

In the tables to be found in the following chapters for the profit target method adapted to three against the field up to six against the field, betting tax is incorporated into all the figures.

4

THE PROFIT TARGET METHOD

THREE AGAINST THE FIELD

The calculations necessary to apply the formula to three or more horses against the field are much more complicated than for just two selections and can only really be done with the aid of a computer. Therefore in all subsequent applications of the *profit target* method a complete computer program is given in each case. The programs are written in WG BASIC and can be used on any modern, IBM compatible microcomputer sold for home use, although the precise wording of the instructions to the computer will vary from make to make.

For everyone, whether they use a computer or not, in the pages that follow there are many *staking tables* which will cover bets on horses priced at all off the more common odds. Also, for those not using a computer Chapters 8 and 9 explain a simpler method with which a full range of bets can be worked out quickly and accurately without a lot of tedious calculation.

With the *profit target* system there are three methods you can employ when you want to back three selections in the same race. For each method I have produced some worked examples, followed by a set of *staking tables* to cover many likely bets. At the end of the book you will find the relevant computer program which I use for my own purposes.

Method 1: Stake to make the same amount of profit when any one of your three selections is the winner.

PROFIT TARGET
THREE AGAINST THE FIELD

Runners	Odds	Stake	Return	Profit
A	3-1	£3.11	£12.44	£5.02
B	5-1	£2.08	£12.48	£5.06
C	7-1	£1.56	£12.48	£5.06
	Stakes	£6.75		
	Tax	£0.67		
	Total outlay	£7.42		

Total outlay £7.42.
Winner Runner A: Profit £5.02.
Winner Runner B: Profit £5.06.
Winner Runner C: Profit £5.06.

PROFIT TARGET
THREE AGAINST THE FIELD

Runners	Odds	Stake	Return	Profit
A	10-1	£3.52	£38.72	£30.15
B	15-1	£2.42	£38.72	£30.15
C	20-1	£1.85	£38.85	£30.28
	Stakes	£7.79		
	Tax	£0.78		
	Total outlay	£8.57		

Total outlay £8.57.
Winner Runner A: Profit £30.15.
Winner Runner B: Profit £30.15.
Winner Runner C: Profit £30.28.

THREE AGAINST THE FIELD
(Profit Target £2)

Odds	Stake	Odds	Stake	Odds	Stake	Tax	Total Outlay
3-1	£1.56	4-1	£1.25	5-1	£1.05	£0.39	£4.25
3-1	£1.45	4-1	£1.16	6-1	£0.83	£0.34	£3.78
3-1	£1.37	4-1	£1.10	7-1	£0.69	£0.32	£3.48
3-1	£1.32	4-1	£1.05	8-1	£0.59	£0.30	£3.26
3-1	£1.28	4-1	£1.02	9-1	£0.52	£0.28	£3.10
3-1	£1.24	4-1	£1.00	10-1	£0.46	£0.27	£2.97
4-1	£0.92	5-1	£0.77	6-1	£0.66	£0.24	£2.59
4-1	£0.88	5-1	£0.74	7-1	£0.55	£0.22	£2.39
4-1	£0.85	5-1	£0.71	8-1	£0.48	£0.20	£2.24
4-1	£0.83	5-1	£0.69	9-1	£0.42	£0.19	£2.13
4-1	£0.82	5-1	£0.68	10-1	£0.38	£0.19	£2.07
5-1	£0.65	6-1	£0.56	7-1	£0.49	£0.17	£1.87
5-1	£0.63	6-1	£0.54	8-1	£0.42	£0.16	£1.75
5-1	£0.62	6-1	£0.53	9-1	£0.37	£0.15	£1.67
5-1	£0.61	6-1	£0.52	10-1	£0.33	£0.15	£1.61
6-1	£0.50	7-1	£0.44	8-1	£0.39	£0.13	£1.46
6-1	£0.49	7-1	£0.43	9-1	£0.35	£0.13	£1.40
6-1	£0.48	7-1	£0.42	10-1	£0.31	£0.12	£1.33
7-1	£0.41	8-1	£0.36	9-1	£0.33	£0.11	£1.21
7-1	£0.40	8-1	£0.36	10-1	£0.29	£0.11	£1.16

THREE AGAINST THE FIELD
(Profit Target £5)

Odds	Stake	Odds	Stake	Odds	Stake	Tax	Total Outlay
3-1	£3.90	4-1	£3.12	5-1	£2.60	£0.96	£10.58
3-1	£3.60	4-1	£2.88	6-1	£2.06	£0.85	£9.39
3-1	£3.41	4-1	£2.73	7-1	£1.71	£0.79	£8.64

THREE AGAINST THE FIELD
(Profit Target £5)

Odds	Stake	Odds	Stake	Odds	Stake	Tax	Total Outlay
3-1	£3.28	4-1	£2.62	8-1	£1.46	£0.74	£8.10
3-1	£3.17	4-1	£2.54	9-1	£1.28	£0.70	£7.69
3-1	£3.10	4-1	£2.48	10-1	£1.13	£0.67	£7.38
4-1	£2.29	5-1	£1.91	6-1	£1.64	£0.58	£6.42
4-1	£2.19	5-1	£1.82	7-1	£1.37	£0.54	£5.92
4-1	£2.12	5-1	£1.77	8-1	£1.18	£0.51	£5.58
4-1	£2.06	5-1	£1.72	9-1	£1.04	£0.48	£5.30
4-1	£2.02	5-1	£1.69	10-1	£0.93	£0.46	£5.10
5-1	£1.61	6-1	£1.38	7-1	£1.21	£0.42	£4.62
5-1	£1.56	6-1	£1.34	8-1	£1.04	£0.39	£4.33
5-1	£1.53	6-1	£1.31	9-1	£0.92	£0.38	£4.14
5-1	£1.50	6-1	£1.29	10-1	£0.82	£0.36	£3.97
6-1	£1.23	7-1	£1.08	8-1	£0.96	£0.33	£3.60
6-1	£1.21	7-1	£1.06	9-1	£0.85	£0.31	£3.43
6-1	£1.19	7-1	£1.04	10-1	£0.76	£0.30	£3.29
7-1	£1.00	8-1	£0.89	9-1	£0.80	£0.27	£2.96
7-1	£0.99	8-1	£0.88	10-1	£0.72	£0.26	£2.85

THREE AGAINST THE FIELD
(Profit Target £20)

Odds	Stake	Odds	Stake	Odds	Stake	Tax	Total Outlay
10-1	£2.38	16-1	£1.54	15-1	£1.64	£0.56	£6.12
10-1	£2.33	16-1	£1.51	20-1	£1.23	£0.51	£5.58
10-1	£2.30	16-1	£1.49	25-1	£0.98	£0.48	£5.25
10-1	£2.28	16-1	£1.48	30-1	£0.82	£0.46	£5.04
10-1	£2.45	12-1	£2.07	15-1	£1.68	£0.62	£6.82
10-1	£2.39	12-1	£2.03	20-1	£1.26	£0.57	£6.25
10-1	£2.36	12-1	£2.00	25-1	£1.01	£0.54	£5.91
10-1	£2.34	12-1	£1.98	30-1	£0.84	£0.52	£5.68

THREE AGAINST THE FIELD
(Profit Target £20)

Odds	Stake	Odds	Stake	Odds	Stake	Tax	Total Outlay
12-1	£1.98	16-1	£1.51	15-1	£1.61	£0.51	£5.61
12-1	£1.94	16-1	£1.48	20-1	£1.20	£0.46	£5.08
12-1	£1.91	16-1	£1.47	25-1	£0.96	£0.43	£4.77
12-1	£1.90	16-1	£1.45	30-1	£0.80	£0.42	£4.57
15-1	£1.55	16-1	£1.46	20-1	£1.18	£0.42	£4.61
15-1	£1.53	16-1	£1.44	25-1	£0.94	£0.39	£4.30
15-1	£1.51	16-1	£1.43	30-1	£0.79	£0.37	£4.10
15-1	£1.50	20-1	£1.15	25-1	£0.93	£0.36	£3.94
15-1	£1.49	20-1	£1.14	30-1	£0.77	£0.34	£3.74
15-1	£1.48	20-1	£1.13	35-1	£0.66	£0.33	£3.60
22-1	£1.02	20-1	£1.12	25-1	£0.91	£0.30	£3.35
22-1	£1.02	20-1	£1.11	30-1	£0.76	£0.29	£3.18
22-1	£1.01	20-1	£1.11	35-1	£0.65	£0.28	£3.05

THREE AGAINST THE FIELD
(Profit Target £50)

Odds	Stake	Odds	Stake	Odds	Stake	Tax	Total Outlay
10-1	£5.94	16-1	£3.85	15-1	£4.09	£1.39	£15.27
10-1	£5.82	16-1	£3.77	20-1	£3.05	£1.26	£13.90
10-1	£5.74	16-1	£3.72	25-1	£2.44	£1.19	£13.09
10-1	£5.69	16-1	£3.69	30-1	£2.03	£1.14	£12.55
12-1	£4.93	16-1	£3.77	15-1	£4.01	£1.27	£13.98
12-1	£4.83	16-1	£3.69	20-1	£2.99	£1.15	£12.66
12-1	£4.77	16-1	£3.65	25-1	£2.39	£1.08	£11.89
12-1	£4.73	16-1	£3.62	30-1	£1.99	£1.03	£11.37
15-1	£3.85	16-1	£3.62	20-1	£2.93	£1.04	£11.44
15-1	£3.80	16-1	£3.58	25-1	£2.34	£0.97	£10.69
15-1	£3.77	16-1	£3.55	30-1	£1.95	£0.93	£10.20
15-1	£3.75	16-1	£3.53	35-1	£1.67	£0.90	£9.85

THREE AGAINST THE FIELD
(Profit Target £50)

Odds	Stake	Odds	Stake	Odds	Stake	Tax	Total Outlay
15-1	£3.77	22-1	£2.63	20-1	£2.88	£0.93	£10.21
15-1	£3.73	22-1	£2.59	25-1	£2.30	£0.86	£9.48
15-1	£3.70	22-1	£2.57	30-1	£1.91	£0.82	£9.00
15-1	£3.67	22-1	£2.56	35-1	£1.64	£0.79	£8.66
20-1	£2.79	22-1	£2.55	25-1	£2.25	£0.76	£8.35
20-1	£2.76	22-1	£2.53	30-1	£1.88	£0.72	£7.89
20-1	£2.75	22-1	£2.51	35-1	£1.61	£0.69	£7.56
20-1	£2.74	22-1	£2.50	40-1	£1.41	£0.67	£7.32

THREE AGAINST THE FIELD
(Profit Target £80)

Odds	Stake	Odds	Stake	Odds	Stake	Tax	Total Outlay
10-1	£9.50	16-1	£6.15	15-1	£6.53	£2.22	£24.40
10-1	£9.30	16-1	£6.02	20-1	£4.88	£2.02	£22.22
10-1	£9.18	16-1	£5.94	25-1	£3.89	£1.90	£20.91
10-1	£9.10	16-1	£5.89	30-1	£3.24	£1.82	£20.05
10-1	£9.35	15-1	£6.43	20-1	£4.90	£2.07	£22.75
10-1	£9.23	15-1	£6.35	25-1	£3.91	£1.95	£21.44
10-1	£9.15	15-1	£6.29	30-1	£3.25	£1.87	£20.56
10-1	£9.09	15-1	£6.25	35-1	£2.79	£1.81	£19.94
15-1	£6.03	22-1	£4.20	20-1	£4.59	£1.48	£16.30
15-1	£5.95	22-1	£4.15	25-1	£3.67	£1.38	£15.15
15-1	£5.91	22-1	£4.11	30-1	£3.05	£1.31	£14.38
15-1	£5.87	22-1	£4.09	35-1	£2.62	£1.26	£13.84
20-1	£4.45	22-1	£4.07	25-1	£3.60	£1.21	£13.33
20-1	£4.42	22-1	£4.03	30-1	£3.00	£1.15	£12.60
20-1	£4.39	22-1	£4.01	35-1	£2.57	£1.10	£12.07
20-1	£4.37	22-1	£3.99	40-1	£2.25	£1.06	£11.67

THREE AGAINST THE FIELD
(Profit Target £100)

Odds	Stake	Odds	Stake	Odds	Stake	Tax	Total Outlay
10-1	£11.68	15-1	£8.03	20-1	£6.12	£2.58	£28.41
10-1	£11.53	15-1	£7.93	25-1	£4.89	£2.44	£26.79
10-1	£11.43	15-1	£7.86	30-1	£4.06	£2.34	£25.69
10-1	£11.36	15-1	£7.82	35-1	£3.48	£2.27	£24.93
10-1	£11.38	22-1	£5.45	20-1	£5.96	£2.28	£25.07
10-1	£11.24	22-1	£5.38	25-1	£4.76	£2.14	£23.52
10-1	£11.14	22-1	£5.33	30-1	£3.96	£2.04	£22.47
10-1	£11.07	22-1	£5.30	35-1	£3.39	£1.98	£21.74
20-1	£5.56	22-1	£5.08	25-1	£4.50	£1.51	£16.65
20-1	£5.52	22-1	£5.04	30-1	£3.74	£1.43	£15.73
20-1	£5.49	22-1	£5.01	35-1	£3.21	£1.37	£15.08
20-1	£5.46	22-1	£4.99	40-1	£2.80	£1.33	£14.58
20-1	£5.53	25-1	£4.47	25-1	£4.47	£1.45	£15.92
20-1	£5.48	25-1	£4.43	30-1	£3.72	£1.36	£14.99
20-1	£5.45	25-1	£4.41	35-1	£3.19	£1.31	£14.36
20-1	£5.43	25-1	£4.39	40-1	£2.79	£1.26	£13.87

Method 2: Stake to produce a graduated profit.

THREE AGAINST THE FIELD

Runners	Odds	Stake	Return	Profit
A	3-1	£2.82	£11.28	£5.05
B	4-1	£2.07	£10.35	£4.12
C	6-1	£1.34	£9.38	£3.15
	Stakes	£6.23		
	Tax	£0.62		
	Total outlay	£6.85		

Total outlay £6.85.

If Runner A wins, profit £5.05.
If Runner B wins, profit £4.12.
If Runner C wins, profit £3.15.

THREE AGAINST THE FIELD

Runners	Odds	Stake	Return	Profit
A	10-1	£5.56	£61.16	£50.41
B	15-1	£3.21	£51.36	£40.61
C	20-1	£1.98	£41.58	£30.83
	Stakes	£10.75		
	Tax	£1.08		
	Total outlay	£11.83		

Total outlay £11.83.
If Runner A wins, profit £50.41.
If Runner B wins, profit £40.61.
If Runner C wins, profit £30.83.

THREE AGAINST THE FIELD

(Profit Target Runner A £20)

(Profit Target Runner B £15)

(Profit Target Runner C £10)

Odds	Stake	Odds	Stake	Odds	Stake	Tax	Total Outlay
10-1	£2.24	15-1	£1.23	20-1	£0.70	£0.41	£4.58
10-1	£2.22	15-1	£1.22	25-1	£0.56	£0.40	£4.40
10-1	£2.21	15-1	£1.21	30-1	£0.46	£0.39	£4.27
10-1	£2.20	15-1	£1.20	35-1	£0.40	£0.38	£4.18
10-1	£2.23	20-1	£0.93	15-1	£0.91	£0.41	£4.48
10-1	£2.20	20-1	£0.92	20-1	£0.68	£0.38	£4.18
10-1	£2.19	20-1	£0.91	25-1	£0.54	£0.36	£4.00
15-1	£1.53	10-1	£1.77	20-1	£0.69	£0.40	£4.39
15-1	£1.52	10-1	£1.75	25-1	£0.55	£0.38	£4.20
15-1	£1.51	10-1	£1.74	30-1	£0.46	£0.37	£4.08
15-1	£1.45	20-1	£0.87	25-1	£0.51	£0.28	£3.11
15-1	£1.44	20-1	£0.86	30-1	£0.42	£0.27	£2.99
15-1	£1.44	20-1	£0.86	35-1	£0.36	£0.27	£2.93

Method 3: Take one of your three selections to be your banker and treat your other two selections to be your danger team.

THREE AGAINST THE FIELD

Runners	Odds	Stake	Return	Profit
A	4-1	£2.71	£13.55	£6.00
B	3-1	£2.64	£10.56	£3.01
C	6-1	£1.51	£10.57	£3.02
	Stakes	£6.86		
	Tax	£0.69		
	Total outlay	£7.55		

Total outlay £7.55.
If Runner A wins, profit £6.00.
If Runner B wins, profit £3.01.
If Runner C wins, profit £3.02.

THREE AGAINST THE FIELD

Runners	Odds	Stake	Return	Profit
A	15-1	£3.72	£59.52	£50.18
B	10-1	£3.13	£34.43	£25.09
C	20-1	£1.64	£34.44	£25.10
	Stakes	£8.49		
	Tax	£0.85		
	Total outlay	£9.34		

Total outlay is £9.34.
If Runner A wins, profit £50.18.
If Runner B wins, profit £25.09.
If Runner C wins, profit £25.10.

THREE AGAINST THE FIELD
(Runner A Profit Target £5)
(Team B/C Profit Target £2)

Odds	Stake	Odds	Stake	Odds	Stake	Tax	Total Outlay
3-1	£2.96	4-1	£1.77	5-1	£1.47	£0.62	£6.82
3-1	£3.60	4-1	£1.63	6-1	£1.17	£0.64	£7.04
3-1	£3.41	4-1	£1.55	7-1	£0.97	£0.59	£6.52
3-1	£3.28	4-1	£1.49	8-1	£0.83	£0.56	£6.16
3-1	£3.17	4-1	£1.44	9-1	£0.73	£0.53	£5.87
3-1	£3.10	4-1	£1.41	10-1	£0.64	£0.52	£5.67
4-1	£1.82	5-1	£1.02	6-1	£0.87	£0.37	£4.08
4-1	£2.19	5-1	£0.98	7-1	£0.73	£0.39	£4.29
4-1	£2.12	5-1	£0.94	8-1	£0.63	£0.37	£4.06
4-1	£2.06	5-1	£0.92	9-1	£0.56	£0.35	£3.89
4-1	£2.02	5-1	£0.90	10-1	£0.50	£0.34	£3.76
5-1	£1.32	6-1	£0.71	7-1	£0.62	£0.27	£2.92
5-1	£1.56	6-1	£0.69	8-1	£0.54	£0.28	£3.07
5-1	£1.53	6-1	£0.67	9-1	£0.47	£0.27	£2.94
5-1	£1.50	6-1	£0.66	10-1	£0.42	£0.26	£2.84
5-1	£1.48	6-1	£0.65	11-1	£0.38	£0.25	£2.76
5-1	£1.46	6-1	£0.64	12-1	£0.35	£0.24	£2.69
6-1	£1.04	7-1	£0.54	8-1	£0.48	£0.21	£2.27
6-1	£1.21	7-1	£0.53	9-1	£0.43	£0.22	£2.39
6-1	£1.19	7-1	£0.52	10-1	£0.38	£0.21	£2.30

THREE AGAINST THE FIELD
(Runner A Profit Target £6)
(Team B/C Profit Target £3)

Odds	Stake	Odds	Stake	Odds	Stake	Tax	Total Outlay
3-1	£3.73	4-1	£2.39	5-1	£1.99	£0.81	£8.92
3-1	£4.32	4-1	£2.21	6-1	£1.58	£0.81	£8.92
3-1	£4.09	4-1	£2.09	7-1	£1.31	£0.75	£8.24

THREE AGAINST THE FIELD
(Runner A Profit Target £6)
(Team B/C Profit Target £3)

Odds	Stake	Odds	Stake	Odds	Stake	Tax	Total Outlay
3-1	£3.93	4-1	£2.01	8-1	£1.12	£0.71	£7.77
3-1	£3.81	4-1	£1.95	9-1	£0.98	£0.67	£7.41
3-1	£3.71	4-1	£1.90	10-1	£0.87	£0.65	£7.13
4-1	£2.28	5-1	£1.40	6-1	£1.20	£0.49	£5.37
4-1	£2.62	5-1	£1.34	7-1	£1.01	£0.50	£5.47
4-1	£2.54	5-1	£1.30	8-1	£0.87	£0.47	£5.18
4-1	£2.48	5-1	£1.26	9-1	£0.76	£0.45	£4.95
4-1	£2.43	5-1	£1.24	10-1	£0.68	£0.44	£4.79
5-1	£1.64	6-1	£0.98	7-1	£0.86	£0.35	£3.83
5-1	£1.87	6-1	£0.95	8-1	£0.74	£0.36	£3.92
5-1	£1.83	6-1	£0.93	9-1	£0.66	£0.34	£3.76
5-1	£1.80	6-1	£0.92	10-1	£0.59	£0.33	£3.64
6-1	£1.29	7-1	£0.75	8-1	£0.67	£0.27	£2.98
6-1	£1.45	7-1	£0.74	9-1	£0.59	£0.28	£3.06
6-1	£1.43	7-1	£0.73	10-1	£0.53	£0.27	£2.96

THREE AGAINST THE FIELD
(Runner A Profit Target £10)
(Team B/C Profit Target £5)

Odds	Stake	Odds	Stake	Odds	Stake	Tax	Total Outlay
3-1	£6.21	4-1	£3.97	5-1	£3.31	£1.35	£14.84
3-1	£5.76	4-1	£2.94	6-1	£2.10	£1.08	£11.88
3-1	£5.45	4-1	£2.79	7-1	£1.74	£1.00	£10.98
3-1	£5.23	4-1	£2.67	8-1	£1.49	£0.94	£10.33
3-1	£5.07	4-1	£2.59	9-1	£1.30	£0.90	£9.86
3-1	£4.95	4-1	£2.53	10-1	£1.15	£0.86	£9.49

THREE AGAINST THE FIELD
(Runner A Profit Target £10)
(Team B/C Profit Target £5)

Odds	Stake	Odds	Stake	Odds	Stake	Tax	Total Outlay
4-1	£3.79	5-1	£2.32	6-1	£1.99	£0.81	£8.91
4-1	£3.49	5-1	£1.78	7-1	£1.34	£0.66	£7.27
4-1	£3.38	5-1	£1.72	8-1	£1.15	£0.63	£6.88
4-1	£3.30	5-1	£1.68	9-1	£1.01	£0.60	£6.59
4-1	£3.23	5-1	£1.65	10-1	£0.90	£0.58	£6.36
5-1	£2.73	6-1	£1.63	7-1	£1.43	£0.58	£6.37
5-1	£2.49	6-1	£1.27	8-1	£0.99	£0.48	£5.23
5-1	£2.44	6-1	£1.24	9-1	£0.87	£0.45	£5.00
5-1	£2.39	6-1	£1.22	10-1	£0.78	£0.44	£4.83
6-1	£2.14	7-1	£1.25	8-1	£1.11	£0.45	£4.95
6-1	£1.93	7-1	£0.98	9-1	£0.79	£0.37	£4.07
6-1	£1.90	7-1	£0.97	10-1	£0.71	£0.36	£3.94

THREE AGAINST THE FIELD
(Runner A Profit Target £20)
(Team B/C Profit Target £10)

Odds	Stake	Odds	Stake	Odds	Stake	Tax	Total Outlay
10-1	£2.26	12-1	£1.14	15-1	£0.93	£0.43	£4.76
10-1	£2.39	12-1	£1.12	20-1	£0.70	£0.42	£4.63
10-1	£2.36	12-1	£1.10	25-1	£0.56	£0.40	£4.42
10-1	£2.34	12-1	£1.09	30-1	£0.46	£0.39	£4.28
10-1	£2.22	16-1	£0.85	15-1	£0.91	£0.40	£4.38
10-1	£2.33	16-1	£0.84	20-1	£0.68	£0.39	£4.24
10-1	£2.30	16-1	£0.83	25-1	£0.54	£0.37	£4.04
10-1	£2.28	16-1	£0.82	30-1	£0.45	£0.36	£3.91

THREE AGAINST THE FIELD
(Runner A Profit Target £20)
(Team B/C Profit Target £10)

Odds	Stake	Odds	Stake	Odds	Stake	Tax	Total Outlay
15-1	£1.46	16-1	£0.78	20-1	£0.64	£0.29	£3.17
15-1	£1.53	16-1	£0.77	25-1	£0.51	£0.28	£3.09
15-1	£1.51	16-1	£0.77	30-1	£0.42	£0.27	£2.97
16-1	£1.38	16-1	£0.79	15-1	£0.84	£0.30	£3.31
16-1	£1.45	16-1	£0.78	20-1	£0.63	£0.29	£3.15
16-1	£1.43	16-1	£0.77	25-1	£0.50	£0.27	£2.97
16-1	£1.42	16-1	£0.76	30-1	£0.42	£0.26	£2.86
20-1	£1.07	22-1	£0.54	25-1	£0.48	£0.21	£2.30
20-1	£1.11	22-1	£0.54	30-1	£0.40	£0.20	£2.25
20-1	£1.11	22-1	£0.54	35-1	£0.35	£0.20	£2.20

THREE AGAINST THE FIELD
(Runner A Profit Target £30)
(Team B/C Profit Target £15)

Odds	Stake	Odds	Stake	Odds	Stake	Tax	Total Outlay
10-1	£3.38	12-1	£1.71	15-1	£1.39	£0.65	£7.13
10-1	£3.58	12-1	£1.67	20-1	£1.04	£0.63	£6.92
10-1	£3.54	12-1	£1.65	25-1	£0.83	£0.60	£6.62
10-1	£3.51	12-1	£1.64	30-1	£0.69	£0.58	£6.42
12-1	£2.84	10-1	£1.99	15-1	£1.37	£0.62	£6.82
12-1	£3.03	10-1	£1.95	20-1	£1.03	£0.60	£6.61
12-1	£3.00	10-1	£1.92	25-1	£0.82	£0.57	£6.31
12-1	£2.97	10-1	£1.91	30-1	£0.68	£0.56	£6.12
16-1	£2.12	10-1	£1.90	15-1	£1.31	£0.53	£5.86
16-1	£2.26	10-1	£1.86	20-1	£0.98	£0.51	£5.61
16-1	£2.24	10-1	£1.84	25-1	£0.78	£0.49	£5.35
16-1	£2.22	10-1	£1.83	30-1	£0.65	£0.47	£5.17

THREE AGAINST THE FIELD
(Runner A Profit Target £30)
(Team B/C Profit Target £15)

Odds	Stake	Odds	Stake	Odds	Stake	Tax	Total Outlay
15-1	£2.15	22-1	£0.85	20-1	£0.93	£0.39	£4.32
15-1	£2.24	22-1	£0.84	25-1	£0.74	£0.38	£4.20
15-1	£2.22	22-1	£0.83	30-1	£0.62	£0.37	£4.04
20-1	£1.60	22-1	£0.81	25-1	£0.72	£0.31	£3.44
20-1	£1.66	22-1	£0.80	30-1	£0.60	£0.31	£3.37
20-1	£1.65	22-1	£0.80	35-1	£0.51	£0.30	£3.26

THREE AGAINST THE FIELD
(Runner A Profit Target £40)
(Team B/C Profit Target £20)

Odds	Stake	Odds	Stake	Odds	Stake	Tax	Total Outlay
10-1	£4.40	15-1	£1.78	20-1	£1.36	£0.75	£8.29
10-1	£4.62	15-1	£1.75	25-1	£1.08	£0.75	£8.20
10-1	£4.58	15-1	£1.74	30-1	£0.90	£0.72	£7.94
10-1	£4.55	15-1	£1.73	35-1	£0.77	£0.70	£7.75
10-1	£4.38	16-1	£1.66	20-1	£1.35	£0.74	£8.13
10-1	£4.60	16-1	£1.64	25-1	£1.08	£0.73	£8.05
10-1	£4.56	16-1	£1.63	30-1	£0.90	£0.71	£7.80
10-1	£4.34	20-1	£1.33	20-1	£1.33	£0.70	£7.70
10-1	£4.53	20-1	£1.31	25-1	£1.06	£0.69	£7.59
10-1	£4.49	20-1	£1.30	30-1	£0.88	£0.67	£7.34
15-1	£2.87	22-1	£1.13	20-1	£1.23	£0.52	£5.75
15-1	£2.98	22-1	£1.11	25-1	£0.99	£0.51	£5.59
15-1	£2.96	22-1	£1.11	30-1	£0.82	£0.49	£5.38
15-1	£2.88	20-1	£1.24	20-1	£1.24	£0.54	£5.90
15-1	£3.00	20-1	£1.23	25-1	£0.99	£0.52	£5.74
15-1	£2.97	20-1	£1.22	30-1	£0.83	£0.50	£5.52

THREE AGAINST THE FIELD
(Runner A Profit Target £40)
(Team B/C Profit Target £20)

Odds	Stake	Odds	Stake	Odds	Stake	Tax	Total Outlay
20-1	£2.13	22-1	£1.08	25-1	£0.95	£0.42	£4.58
20-1	£2.21	22-1	£1.07	30-1	£0.80	£0.41	£4.49
20-1	£2.20	22-1	£1.06	35-1	£0.68	£0.39	£4.33
20-1	£2.14	20-1	£1.19	25-1	£0.96	£0.43	£4.72
20-1	£2.23	20-1	£1.18	30-1	£0.80	£0.42	£4.63
20-1	£2.21	20-1	£1.17	35-1	£0.69	£0.41	£4.48

THREE AGAINST THE FIELD
(Runner A Profit Target £50)
(Team B/C Profit Target £25)

Odds	Stake	Odds	Stake	Odds	Stake	Tax	Total Outlay
10-1	£5.45	16-1	£2.12	15-1	£2.25	£0.99	£10.90
10-1	£5.82	16-1	£2.08	20-1	£1.68	£0.96	£10.54
10-1	£5.74	16-1	£2.05	25-1	£1.34	£0.91	£10.04
10-1	£5.69	16-1	£2.03	30-1	£1.12	£0.88	£9.72
15-1	£3.67	16-1	£1.98	15-1	£2.10	£0.78	£8.53
15-1	£3.85	16-1	£1.94	20-1	£1.57	£0.74	£8.10
15-1	£3.80	16-1	£1.92	25-1	£1.26	£0.70	£7.68
15-1	£3.77	16-1	£1.90	30-1	£1.05	£0.67	£7.39
16-1	£3.44	15-1	£2.10	15-1	£2.10	£0.76	£8.40
16-1	£3.62	15-1	£2.05	20-1	£1.57	£0.72	£7.96
16-1	£3.58	15-1	£2.03	25-1	£1.25	£0.69	£7.55
16-1	£3.55	15-1	£2.01	30-1	£1.04	£0.66	£7.26

THREE AGAINST THE FIELD
(Runner A Profit Target £50)
(Team B/C Profit Target £25)

Odds	Stake	Odds	Stake	Odds	Stake	Tax	Total Outlay
15-1	£3.57	20-1	£1.53	25-1	£1.24	£0.63	£6.97
15-1	£3.72	20-1	£1.52	30-1	£1.03	£0.63	£6.90
15-1	£3.69	20-1	£1.51	35-1	£0.88	£0.61	£6.69
15-1	£3.68	20-1	£1.50	40-1	£0.77	£0.60	£6.55
22-1	£2.44	20-1	£1.48	20-1	£1.48	£0.54	£5.94
22-1	£2.55	20-1	£1.46	25-1	£1.18	£0.52	£5.71
22-1	£2.53	20-1	£1.45	30-1	£0.99	£0.50	£5.47
22-1	£2.51	20-1	£1.45	35-1	£0.85	£0.48	£5.29

THREE AGAINST THE FIELD
(Runner A Profit Target £100)
(Team B/C Profit Target £50)

Odds	Stake	Odds	Stake	Odds	Stake	Tax	Total Outlay
10-1	£11.08	16-1	£4.23	15-1	£4.49	£1.98	£21.78
10-1	£11.62	16-1	£4.14	20-1	£3.36	£1.91	£21.03
10-1	£11.47	16-1	£4.09	25-1	£2.68	£1.82	£20.06
10-1	£11.38	16-1	£4.06	30-1	£2.23	£1.77	£19.44
15-1	£7.32	16-1	£3.95	15-1	£4.20	£1.55	£17.02
15-1	£7.69	16-1	£3.87	20-1	£3.14	£1.47	£16.17
15-1	£7.59	16-1	£3.82	25-1	£2.50	£1.39	£15.30
15-1	£7.53	16-1	£3.79	30-1	£2.08	£1.34	£14.74
15-1	£7.26	15-1	£4.13	20-1	£3.15	£1.45	£15.99
15-1	£7.63	15-1	£4.08	25-1	£2.52	£1.42	£15.65
15-1	£7.57	15-1	£4.05	30-1	£2.09	£1.37	£15.08
15-1	£7.52	15-1	£4.02	35-1	£1.79	£1.33	£14.66

THREE AGAINST THE FIELD
(Runner A Profit Target £100)
(Team B/C Profit Target £50)

Odds	Stake	Odds	Stake	Odds	Stake	Tax	Total Outlay
20-1	£5.47	16-1	£3.81	15-1	£4.05	£1.33	£14.66
20-1	£5.74	16-1	£3.74	20-1	£3.03	£1.25	£13.76
20-1	£5.67	16-1	£3.69	25-1	£2.42	£1.18	£12.96
20-1	£5.63	16-1	£3.66	30-1	£2.01	£1.13	£12.43
22-1	£4.87	20-1	£2.95	20-1	£2.95	£1.08	£11.85
22-1	£5.08	20-1	£2.92	25-1	£2.36	£1.04	£11.40
22-1	£5.04	20-1	£2.90	30-1	£1.97	£0.99	£10.90
22-1	£5.01	20-1	£2.88	35-1	£1.68	£0.96	£10.53

5

THE PROFIT TARGET METHOD

FOUR AGAINST
THE FIELD

Method 1: Stake on four runners in the same event so that if any one of the four is the winner you make a predetermined profit.

FOUR AGAINST THE FIELD

Runners	Odds	Stake	Return	Profit
A	15-1	£3.90	£62.40	£50.18
B	20-1	£2.97	£62.37	£50.15
C	25-1	£2.40	£62.40	£50.18
D	33-1	£1.84	£62.56	£50.34
	Stakes	£11.11		
	Tax	£1.11		
	Total outlay	£12.22		

Total outlay £12.22.

If any one of the four selections is the winner you will recoup the total outlay and make a net profit of £50.

FOUR AGAINST THE FIELD
(Profit Target £20)

Odds	Stake	Odds	Stake	Odds	Stake	Odds	Stake	Total Outlay
10-1	£2.63	12-1	£2.22	15-1	£1.81	20-1	£1.38	£8.84
10-1	£2.59	12-1	£2.20	15-1	£1.79	25-1	£1.10	£8.45
10-1	£2.57	12-1	£2.18	15-1	£1.77	30-1	£0.92	£8.18
10-1	£2.55	12-1	£2.16	15-1	£1.76	35-1	£0.79	£7.99
10-1	£2.68	12-1	£2.27	16-1	£1.74	15-1	£1.85	£9.39
10-1	£2.61	12-1	£2.22	16-1	£1.70	20-1	£1.38	£8.70
10-1	£2.58	12-1	£2.18	16-1	£1.67	25-1	£1.10	£8.28
10-1	£2.55	12-1	£2.16	16-1	£1.66	30-1	£0.91	£8.01
15-1	£1.64	16-1	£1.55	22-1	£1.14	20-1	£1.25	£6.14
15-1	£1.62	16-1	£1.53	22-1	£1.13	25-1	£1.00	£5.81
15-1	£1.61	16-1	£1.51	22-1	£1.12	30-1	£0.83	£5.58
15-1	£1.56	20-1	£1.19	33-1	£0.74	25-1	£0.97	£4.91
15-1	£1.55	20-1	£1.18	33-1	£0.74	30-1	£0.81	£4.71
15-1	£1.54	20-1	£1.18	33-1	£0.73	35-1	£0.69	£4.55
20-1	£1.16	22-1	£1.06	33-1	£0.72	25-1	£0.94	£4.27
20-1	£1.15	22-1	£1.06	33-1	£0.72	30-1	£0.79	£4.09
20-1	£1.15	22-1	£1.05	33-1	£0.71	35-1	£0.67	£3.94

Note: total outlay = stakes plus tax.

FOUR AGAINST THE FIELD
(Profit Target £30)

Odds	Stake	Odds	Stake	Odds	Stake	Odds	Stake	Total Outlay
10-1	£4.01	12-1	£3.40	16-1	£2.60	15-1	£2.76	£14.05
10-1	£3.92	12-1	£3.32	16-1	£2.54	20-1	£2.06	£13.02
10-1	£3.86	12-1	£3.27	16-1	£2.50	25-1	£1.64	£12.40
10-1	£3.82	12-1	£3.24	16-1	£2.48	30-1	£1.36	£11.99
10-1	£3.94	12-1	£3.33	15-1	£2.71	20-1	£2.07	£13.26
10-1	£3.88	12-1	£3.29	15-1	£2.67	25-1	£1.65	£12.64
10-1	£3.85	12-1	£3.26	15-1	£2.65	30-1	£1.37	£12.24

FOUR AGAINST THE FIELD
(Profit Target £30)

Odds	Stake	Odds	Stake	Odds	Stake	Odds	Stake	Total Outlay
15-1	£2.46	16-1	£2.31	22-1	£1.71	20-1	£1.87	£9.18
15-1	£2.43	16-1	£2.28	22-1	£1.69	25-1	£1.50	£8.69
15-1	£2.40	16-1	£2.26	22-1	£1.68	30-1	£1.25	£8.35
15-1	£2.34	20-1	£1.79	33-1	£1.11	25-1	£1.44	£7.35
15-1	£2.32	20-1	£1.77	33-1	£1.10	30-1	£1.20	£7.03
15-1	£2.31	20-1	£1.76	33-1	£1.09	35-1	£1.03	£6.81
20-1	£1.76	22-1	£1.61	25-1	£1.42	25-1	£1.42	£6.83
20-1	£1.75	22-1	£1.60	25-1	£1.41	30-1	£1.19	£6.55
20-1	£1.74	22-1	£1.59	25-1	£1.41	35-1	£1.02	£6.34

Note: total outlay = stakes plus tax.

FOUR AGAINST THE FIELD
(Profit Target £50)

Odds	Stake	Odds	Stake	Odds	Stake	Odds	Stake	Total Outlay
10-1	£6.68	12-1	£5.66	16-1	£4.33	15-1	£4.60	£23.40
10-1	£6.52	12-1	£5.52	16-1	£4.23	20-1	£3.42	£21.66
10-1	£6.43	12-1	£5.44	16-1	£4.16	25-1	£2.72	£20.63
10-1	£6.37	12-1	£5.39	16-1	£4.12	30-1	£2.27	£19.96
10-1	£6.37	15-1	£4.38	16-1	£4.13	20-1	£3.34	£20.04
10-1	£6.29	15-1	£4.32	16-1	£4.07	25-1	£2.66	£19.07
10-1	£6.23	15-1	£4.29	16-1	£4.03	30-1	£2.22	£18.45
15-1	£4.09	16-1	£3.85	22-1	£2.85	20-1	£3.12	£15.30
15-1	£4.04	16-1	£3.80	22-1	£2.81	25-1	£2.49	£14.45
15-1	£4.00	16-1	£3.77	22-1	£2.79	30-1	£2.07	£13.89
15-1	£3.94	20-1	£3.01	25-1	£2.43	25-1	£2.43	£12.99
15-1	£3.91	20-1	£2.98	25-1	£2.41	30-1	£2.02	£12.45
15-1	£3.89	20-1	£2.97	25-1	£2.40	35-1	£1.73	£12.09

FOUR AGAINST THE FIELD
(Profit Target £50)

Odds	Stake	Odds	Stake	Odds	Stake	Odds	Stake	Total Outlay
20-1	£2.90	22-1	£2.64	33-1	£1.79	25-1	£2.34	£10.64
20-1	£2.87	22-1	£2.62	33-1	£1.78	30-1	£1.95	£10.14
20-1	£2.86	22-1	£2.61	33-1	£1.77	35-1	£1.67	£9.80

Note: total outlay = stakes plus tax.

Method 2: Stake on one runner to be your main selection to produce your best profit target. At the same time stake on team B/C/D as your danger team to produce a less profit target.

FOUR AGAINST THE FIELD

Runners	Odds	Stake	Return	Profit
A	20-1	£3.25	£68.25	£60.20
B	25-1	£1.47	£38.22	£30.17
C	25-1	£1.47	£38.22	£30.17
D	33-1	£1.13	£38.42	£30.37
	Stakes	£7.32		
	Tax	£0.73		
	Total outlay	£8.05		

Total outlay £8.05.
If Runner A wins, net profit £60.
If Runner B, C or D wins, net profit £30.

FOUR AGAINST THE FIELD
(Runner A Profit Target £50)
(Team B/C/D Profit Target £25)

Odds	Stake	Odds	Stake	Odds	Stake	Odds	Stake	Total Outlay
10-1	£5.95	12-1	£3.12	16-1	£2.38	15-1	£2.53	£15.38
10-1	£5.86	12-1	£3.04	16-1	£2.33	20-1	£1.89	£14.43
10-1	£5.81	12-1	£3.00	16-1	£2.29	25-1	£1.50	£13.86
10-1	£5.78	12-1	£2.97	16-1	£2.27	30-1	£1.25	£13.50
10-1	£5.78	15-1	£2.42	16-1	£2.27	20-1	£1.84	£13.54
10-1	£5.73	15-1	£2.38	16-1	£2.24	25-1	£1.47	£13.00
10-1	£5.70	15-1	£2.36	16-1	£2.22	30-1	£1.22	£12.65
10-1	£5.70	15-1	£2.36	22-1	£1.65	20-1	£1.80	£12.66
10-1	£5.66	15-1	£2.33	22-1	£1.62	25-1	£1.44	£12.16
10-1	£5.63	15-1	£2.31	22-1	£1.61	30-1	£1.20	£11.83
10-1	£5.68	15-1	£2.34	20-1	£1.79	25-1	£1.45	£12.39
10-1	£5.65	15-1	£2.32	20-1	£1.77	30-1	£1.20	£12.03
10-1	£5.62	15-1	£2.31	20-1	£1.76	35-1	£1.03	£11.79
15-1	£3.65	20-1	£1.59	33-1	£0.99	25-1	£1.29	£8.27
15-1	£3.63	20-1	£1.58	33-1	£0.98	30-1	£1.07	£7.99
15-1	£3.62	20-1	£1.57	33-1	£0.97	35-1	£0.92	£7.79

Note: total outlay = stakes plus tax.

FOUR AGAINST THE FIELD
(Runner A Profit Target £60)
(Team B/C/D Profit Target £20)

Odds	Stake	Odds	Stake	Odds	Stake	Odds	Stake	Total Outlay
10-1	£6.63	15-1	£2.06	22-1	£1.44	20-1	£1.57	£12.87
10-1	£6.59	15-1	£2.04	22-1	£1.42	25-1	£1.26	£12.44
10-1	£6.56	15-1	£2.02	22-1	£1.41	30-1	£1.05	£12.14
10-1	£6.54	15-1	£2.00	22-1	£1.40	35-1	£0.89	£11.91

FOUR AGAINST THE FIELD
(Runner A Profit Target £60)
(Team B/C/D Profit Target £20)

Odds	Stake	Odds	Stake	Odds	Stake	Odds	Stake	Total Outlay
10-1	£6.61	15-1	£2.05	20-1	£1.56	25-1	£1.26	£12.63
10-1	£6.58	15-1	£2.03	20-1	£1.55	30-1	£1.05	£12.33
10-1	£6.56	15-1	£2.02	20-1	£1.54	35-1	£0.90	£12.13
10-1	£6.55	15-1	£2.01	20-1	£1.53	40-1	£0.79	£11.97
15-1	£4.38	16-1	£1.77	20-1	£1.43	20-1	£1.43	£9.91
15-1	£4.35	16-1	£1.74	20-1	£1.41	25-1	£1.14	£9.50
15-1	£4.34	16-1	£1.73	20-1	£1.40	30-1	£0.95	£9.26
15-1	£4.32	16-1	£1.72	20-1	£1.39	35-1	£0.82	£9.08
15-1	£4.28	20-1	£1.36	33-1	£0.84	25-1	£1.10	£8.34
15-1	£4.26	20-1	£1.35	33-1	£0.84	30-1	£0.91	£8.10
15-1	£4.25	20-1	£1.34	33-1	£0.83	35-1	£0.78	£7.92
15-1	£4.24	20-1	£1.33	33-1	£0.83	40-1	£0.69	£7.80

Note: total outlay = stakes plus tax.

FOUR AGAINST THE FIELD
(Runner A Profit Target £100)
(Team B/C/D Profit Target £10)

Odds	Stake	Odds	Stake	Odds	Stake	Odds	Stake	Total Outlay
10-1	£10.54	15-1	£1.62	20-1	£1.24	25-1	£1.00	£15.84
10-1	£10.52	15-1	£1.61	20-1	£1.23	30-1	£0.83	£15.61
10-1	£10.50	15-1	£1.60	20-1	£1.22	35-1	£0.72	£15.44
10-1	£10.49	15-1	£1.59	20-1	£1.21	40-1	£0.63	£15.31
15-1	£6.92	20-1	£0.99	22-1	£0.90	25-1	£0.80	£10.57
15-1	£6.91	20-1	£0.98	22-1	£0.89	30-1	£0.67	£10.40
15-1	£6.90	20-1	£0.97	22-1	£0.89	35-1	£0.57	£10.26
15-1	£6.89	20-1	£0.97	22-1	£0.89	40-1	£0.50	£10.18

FOUR AGAINST THE FIELD
(Runner A Profit Target £100)
(Team B/C/D Profit Target £10)

Odds	Stake	Odds	Stake	Odds	Stake	Odds	Stake	Total Outlay
20-1	£5.14	25-1	£0.69	33-1	£0.53	25-1	£0.69	£7.76
20-1	£5.13	25-1	£0.69	33-1	£0.53	30-1	£0.58	£7.62
20-1	£5.13	25-1	£0.68	33-1	£0.52	35-1	£0.50	£7.51
20-1	£5.12	25-1	£0.68	33-1	£0.52	40-1	£0.43	£7.43

Note: total outlay = stakes plus tax.

Method 3: Split your selections into two teams: team A/B to produce your best profit target; team C/D, your danger team, to produce a lesser profit target.

FOUR AGAINST THE FIELD

Runners	Odds	Stake	Return	Profit
A	15-1	£3.75	£60.00	£50.10
B	20-1	£2.86	£60.06	£50.16
C	25-1	£1.35	£35.10	£25.20
D	33-1	£1.04	£35.36	£25.46
	Stakes	£9.00		
	Tax	£0.90		
	Total outlay	£9.90		

Total outlay £9.90.
If Runner A wins, profit £50.10.
If Runner B wins, profit £50.16.
If Runner C wins, profit £25.20.
If Runner D wins, profit £25.46.

FOUR AGAINST THE FIELD
(Team A/B Profit Target £20)
(Team C/D Profit Target £10)

Odds	Stake	Odds	Stake	Odds	Stake	Odds	Stake	Total Outlay
8-1	£3.46	10-1	£2.83	16-1	£1.13	15-1	£1.20	£9.48
8-1	£3.18	10-1	£2.60	16-1	£1.10	20-1	£0.89	£8.55
8-1	£3.15	10-1	£2.58	16-1	£1.08	25-1	£0.71	£8.27
8-1	£3.13	10-1	£2.56	16-1	£1.07	30-1	£0.59	£8.09
10-1	£2.68	12-1	£2.27	16-1	£1.03	15-1	£1.10	£7.79
10-1	£2.46	12-1	£2.08	16-1	£1.01	20-1	£0.82	£7.01
10-1	£2.44	12-1	£2.07	16-1	£0.99	25-1	£0.65	£6.77
10-1	£2.42	12-1	£2.05	16-1	£0.98	30-1	£0.54	£6.59
15-1	£1.58	20-1	£1.21	25-1	£0.55	25-1	£0.55	£4.28
15-1	£1.51	20-1	£1.15	25-1	£0.55	30-1	£0.46	£4.04
15-1	£1.50	20-1	£1.15	25-1	£0.54	35-1	£0.40	£3.95
15-1	£1.50	20-1	£1.15	25-1	£0.54	40-1	£0.35	£3.89
15-1	£1.56	20-1	£1.19	33-1	£0.42	25-1	£0.55	£4.09
15-1	£1.50	20-1	£1.14	33-1	£0.42	30-1	£0.46	£3.87
15-1	£1.49	20-1	£1.14	33-1	£0.41	35-1	£0.39	£3.77
15-1	£1.49	20-1	£1.14	33-1	£0.41	40-1	£0.34	£3.72
20-1	£1.16	25-1	£0.94	25-1	£0.52	30-1	£0.44	£3.37
20-1	£1.11	25-1	£0.90	25-1	£0.52	35-1	£0.38	£3.20
20-1	£1.11	25-1	£0.90	25-1	£0.51	40-1	£0.33	£3.14

Note: total outlay = stakes plus tax.

FOUR AGAINST THE FIELD
(Team A/B Profit Target £50)
(Team C/D Profit Target £25)

Odds	Stake	Odds	Stake	Odds	Stake	Odds	Stake	Total Outlay
10-1	£6.18	15-1	£4.25	20-1	£1.90	25-1	£1.54	£15.26
10-1	£5.86	15-1	£4.03	20-1	£1.88	30-1	£1.28	£14.35
10-1	£5.83	15-1	£4.01	20-1	£1.87	35-1	£1.09	£14.08
10-1	£5.81	15-1	£4.00	20-1	£1.86	40-1	£0.96	£13.89
10-1	£6.18	20-1	£3.24	15-1	£2.45	25-1	£1.51	£14.72
10-1	£5.81	20-1	£3.05	15-1	£2.43	30-1	£1.26	£13.81
10-1	£5.78	20-1	£3.03	15-1	£2.42	35-1	£1.08	£13.54
10-1	£5.77	20-1	£3.02	15-1	£2.40	40-1	£0.94	£13.34
15-1	£4.00	20-1	£3.05	20-1	£1.71	25-1	£1.38	£11.15
15-1	£3.79	20-1	£2.89	20-1	£1.70	30-1	£1.15	£10.48
15-1	£3.77	20-1	£2.88	20-1	£1.69	35-1	£0.99	£10.26
15-1	£3.76	20-1	£2.87	20-1	£1.68	40-1	£0.86	£10.09
15-1	£3.90	25-1	£2.40	33-1	£1.03	20-1	£1.65	£9.88
15-1	£3.70	25-1	£2.28	33-1	£1.01	25-1	£1.32	£9.14
15-1	£3.69	25-1	£2.27	33-1	£1.00	30-1	£1.10	£8.87
15-1	£3.67	25-1	£2.26	33-1	£1.00	35-1	£0.94	£8.66
20-1	£3.24	25-1	£2.62	10-1	£3.39	15-1	£2.33	£12.74
20-1	£2.93	25-1	£2.37	10-1	£3.31	20-1	£1.74	£11.39
20-1	£2.91	25-1	£2.35	10-1	£3.27	25-1	£1.39	£10.91
20-1	£2.89	25-1	£2.34	10-1	£3.24	30-1	£1.16	£10.59

Note: total outlay = stakes plus tax.

FOUR AGAINST THE FIELD
(Team A/B Profit Target £100)
(Team C/D Profit Target £10)

Odds	Stake	Odds	Stake	Odds	Stake	Odds	Stake	Total Outlay
15-1	£7.78	20-1	£5.93	33-1	£0.77	25-1	£1.01	£17.04
15-1	£7.25	20-1	£5.52	33-1	£0.77	30-1	£0.84	£15.82
15-1	£7.24	20-1	£5.52	33-1	£0.76	35-1	£0.72	£15.66
15-1	£7.23	20-1	£5.51	33-1	£0.76	40-1	£0.63	£15.54
15-1	£7.88	25-1	£4.85	20-1	£1.21	25-1	£0.98	£16.41
15-1	£7.20	25-1	£4.43	20-1	£1.20	30-1	£0.82	£15.01
15-1	£7.19	25-1	£4.43	20-1	£1.19	35-1	£0.70	£14.86
15-1	£7.18	25-1	£4.42	20-1	£1.19	40-1	£0.61	£14.74
20-1	£6.48	25-1	£5.23	15-1	£1.58	10-1	£2.30	£17.15
20-1	£5.44	25-1	£4.40	15-1	£1.52	15-1	£1.52	£14.17
20-1	£5.42	25-1	£4.38	15-1	£1.49	20-1	£1.13	£13.66
20-1	£5.41	25-1	£4.37	15-1	£1.47	25-1	£0.91	£13.38
20-1	£5.40	25-1	£4.36	15-1	£1.46	30-1	£0.76	£13.18
25-1	£4.79	33-1	£3.67	20-1	£1.00	15-1	£1.31	£11.85
25-1	£4.26	33-1	£3.26	20-1	£0.98	20-1	£0.98	£10.43
25-1	£4.25	33-1	£3.25	20-1	£0.97	25-1	£0.78	£10.18
25-1	£4.24	33-1	£3.24	20-1	£0.96	30-1	£0.65	£10.00

Note: total outlay = stakes plus tax.

6

THE PROFIT TARGET METHOD

FIVE AGAINST
THE FIELD

Method 1: Stake on five runners in the same event so that you make the same amount of profit whichever one wins.

THE DERBY 1989
Ante Post Odds, September 1988

A	High Estate	25-1
B	Really Brilliant	25-1
C	Nashwan	20-1
D	Observation Post	33-1
E	Prince of Dance	16-1

FIVE AGAINST THE FIELD (Profit Target £50)

Runners	Odds	Stake	Return	Profit
A	25-1	£2.52	£65.52	£50.19
B	25-1	£2.52	£65.52	£50.19
C	20-1	£3.12	£65.52	£50.19
D	33-1	£1.93	£65.62	£50.29
E	16-1	£3.85	£65.45	£50.12
	Stakes	£13.94		
	Tax	£1.39		
	Total outlay	£15.33		

Total outlay £15.33. Nashwan won, profit £50.19.

FIVE AGAINST THE FIELD
(Profit Target £50)

Odds	Stake	Odds	Stake	Odds	Stake	Odds	Stake	Odds	Stake	Total Outlay
15-1	£4.17	20-1	£3.18	20-1	£3.18	33-1	£1.97	25-1	£2.57	£16.58
15-1	£4.13	20-1	£3.15	20-1	£3.15	33-1	£1.95	30-1	£2.14	£15.97
15-1	£4.10	20-1	£3.13	20-1	£3.13	33-1	£1.94	35-1	£1.83	£15.54
15-1	£4.08	20-1	£3.11	20-1	£3.11	33-1	£1.93	40-1	£1.60	£15.21
15-1	£4.24	16-1	£3.99	20-1	£3.23	33-1	£2.00	25-1	£2.61	£17.68
15-1	£4.20	16-1	£3.95	20-1	£3.20	33-1	£1.98	30-1	£2.17	£17.05
15-1	£4.17	16-1	£3.93	20-1	£3.18	33-1	£1.97	35-1	£1.86	£16.62
15-1	£4.15	16-1	£3.91	20-1	£3.16	33-1	£1.96	40-1	£1.63	£16.29
20-1	£3.11	20-1	£3.11	25-1	£2.51	25-1	£2.51	25-1	£2.51	£15.12
20-1	£3.08	20-1	£3.08	25-1	£2.49	25-1	£2.49	30-1	£2.09	£14.55
20-1	£3.06	20-1	£3.06	25-1	£2.48	25-1	£2.48	35-1	£1.79	£14.16
20-1	£3.05	20-1	£3.05	25-1	£2.46	25-1	£2.46	40-1	£1.57	£13.85
16-1	£3.85	20-1	£3.12	25-1	£2.52	33-1	£1.93	25-1	£2.52	£15.33
16-1	£3.82	20-1	£3.09	25-1	£2.50	33-1	£1.91	30-1	£2.10	£14.76
16-1	£3.79	20-1	£3.07	25-1	£2.48	33-1	£1.90	35-1	£1.80	£14.34
16-1	£3.77	20-1	£3.06	25-1	£2.47	33-1	£1.89	40-1	£1.57	£14.04
20-1	£3.05	22-1	£2.79	25-1	£2.47	33-1	£1.89	25-1	£2.47	£13.94
20-1	£3.03	22-1	£2.76	25-1	£2.45	33-1	£1.87	30-1	£2.05	£13.38
20-1	£3.01	22-1	£2.75	25-1	£2.43	33-1	£1.86	35-1	£1.76	£12.99
20-1	£2.99	22-1	£2.73	25-1	£2.42	33-1	£1.85	40-1	£1.54	£12.68

Note: total outlay = stakes plus tax.

Method 2: Stake on your most fancied runner to make a set profit and also stake on the other four selections to produce a lesser profit target.

FIVE AGAINST THE FIELD

Runners	Odds	Stake	Return	Profit
A	15-1	£4.52	£72.32	£60.18
B	20-1	£2.01	£42.21	£30.07
C	25-1	£1.63	£42.38	£30.24
D	25-1	£1.63	£42.38	£30.24
E	33-1	£1.25	£42.50	£30.36
	Stakes	£11.04		
	Tax	£1.10		
	Total outlay	£12.14		

Total outlay £12.14.

If Runner A wins, profit £60.18.

If Runner B wins, profit £30.07.

If Runner C wins, profit £30.24.

If Runner D wins, profit £30.24.

If Runner E wins, profit £30.36.

FIVE AGAINST THE FIELD
(Profit A @ £40. Profits B/C/D/E @ £10)

Odds	Stake	Odds	Stake	Odds	Stake	Odds	Stake	Odds	Stake	Total Outlay
10-1	£4.46	15-1	£1.20	20-1	£0.91	20-1	£0.91	25-1	£0.74	£9.04
10-1	£4.45	15-1	£1.19	20-1	£0.91	20-1	£0.91	30-1	£0.62	£8.89
10-1	£4.44	15-1	£1.18	20-1	£0.90	20-1	£0.90	35-1	£0.53	£8.75
10-1	£4.68	15-1	£1.91	20-1	£1.46	25-1	£1.18	25-1	£1.18	£11.45
10-1	£4.66	15-1	£1.89	20-1	£1.44	25-1	£1.17	30-1	£0.98	£11.15
10-1	£4.64	15-1	£1.88	20-1	£1.43	25-1	£1.16	35-1	£0.84	£10.95
15-1	£2.90	20-1	£0.78	20-1	£0.78	25-1	£0.64	25-1	£0.64	£6.31
15-1	£2.89	20-1	£0.78	20-1	£0.78	25-1	£0.63	30-1	£0.53	£6.17
15-1	£2.89	20-1	£0.77	20-1	£0.77	25-1	£0.63	35-1	£0.45	£6.06

Note: total outlay = stakes plus tax.

FIVE AGAINST THE FIELD
(Runner A Profit Target £60)
(Team B/C/D/E Profit Target £30)

Odds	Stake	Odds	Stake	Odds	Stake	Odds	Stake	Odds	Stake	Total Outlay
15-1	£4.52	20-1	£2.01	25-1	£1.63	33-1	£1.25	25-1	£1.63	£12.14
15-1	£4.49	20-1	£2.00	25-1	£1.61	33-1	£1.24	30-1	£1.36	£11.77
15-1	£4.48	20-1	£1.98	25-1	£1.60	33-1	£1.23	35-1	£1.16	£11.50
15-1	£4.46	20-1	£1.97	25-1	£1.60	33-1	£1.22	40-1	£1.02	£11.30
20-1	£3.41	15-1	£2.60	25-1	£1.60	33-1	£1.23	25-1	£1.60	£11.48
20-1	£3.39	15-1	£2.58	25-1	£1.59	33-1	£1.22	30-1	£1.33	£11.12
20-1	£3.38	15-1	£2.56	25-1	£1.58	33-1	£1.21	35-1	£1.14	£10.86
20-1	£3.37	15-1	£2.55	25-1	£1.57	33-1	£1.20	40-1	£1.00	£10.66
25-1	£2.74	15-1	£2.58	20-1	£1.96	33-1	£1.22	25-1	£1.59	£11.10
25-1	£2.73	15-1	£2.55	20-1	£1.95	33-1	£1.21	30-1	£1.32	£10.74
25-1	£2.72	15-1	£2.54	20-1	£1.93	33-1	£1.20	35-1	£1.13	£10.47
25-1	£2.71	15-1	£2.52	20-1	£1.93	33-1	£1.19	40-1	£0.99	£10.27
10-1	£7.06	15-1	£2.98	20-1	£2.27	25-1	£1.84	25-1	£1.84	£17.59
10-1	£7.02	15-1	£2.95	20-1	£2.25	25-1	£1.82	30-1	£1.53	£17.13
10-1	£6.99	15-1	£2.93	20-1	£2.24	25-1	£1.81	35-1	£1.31	£16.81
10-1	£6.96	15-1	£2.92	20-1	£2.22	25-1	£1.80	40-1	£1.14	£16.54

Note: total outlay = stakes plus tax.

Method 3. Take your two best selections as your banker team and stake on the other three selections as the danger team.

FIVE AGAINST THE FIELD
(Team A/B Profit Target £60)
(Team C/D/E Profit Target £30)

Runners	Odds	Stake	Return	Profit
A	20-1	£3.49	£73.29	£60.13
B	25-1	£2.82	£73.32	£60.16

C	15-1	£2.70	£43.20	£30.04
D	25-1	£1.67	£43.42	£30.26
E	33-1	£1.28	£43.52	£30.36
	Stakes	£11.96		
	Tax	£1.20		
	Total outlay	£13.16		

Total outlay £13.16.
If Runner A wins, profit £60.13.
If Runner B wins, profit £60.16.
If Runner C wins, profit £30.04.
If Runner D wins, profit £30.26.
If Runner E wins, profit £30.36.

FIVE AGAINST THE FIELD
(Team A/B Profit Target £60)
(Team C/D/E Profit Target £30)

Odds	Stake	Odds	Stake	Odds	Stake	Odds	Stake	Odds	Stake	Total Outlay
15-1	£4.64	20-1	£3.54	25-1	£1.71	33-1	£1.31	25-1	£1.71	£14.20
15-1	£4.62	20-1	£3.52	25-1	£1.69	33-1	£1.30	30-1	£1.42	£13.81
15-1	£4.60	20-1	£3.51	25-1	£1.68	33-1	£1.29	35-1	£1.22	£13.53
15-1	£4.59	20-1	£3.50	25-1	£1.67	33-1	£1.28	40-1	£1.07	£13.32
20-1	£3.49	25-1	£2.82	15-1	£2.70	33-1	£1.28	25-1	£1.67	£13.16
20-1	£3.47	25-1	£2.81	15-1	£2.68	33-1	£1.27	30-1	£1.39	£12.78
20-1	£3.46	25-1	£2.80	15-1	£2.66	33-1	£1.26	35-1	£1.19	£12.51
20-1	£3.45	25-1	£2.79	15-1	£2.65	33-1	£1.25	40-1	£1.04	£12.30
15-1	£4.62	25-1	£2.85	20-1	£2.09	33-1	£1.30	25-1	£1.69	£13.81
15-1	£4.59	25-1	£2.83	20-1	£2.07	33-1	£1.29	30-1	£1.41	£13.41
15-1	£4.58	25-1	£2.82	20-1	£2.06	33-1	£1.28	35-1	£1.21	£13.15
15-1	£4.56	25-1	£2.81	20-1	£2.05	33-1	£1.27	40-1	£1.06	£12.93
16-1	£4.35	20-1	£3.52	25-1	£1.69	33-1	£1.30	25-1	£1.69	£13.81
16-1	£4.33	20-1	£3.50	25-1	£1.68	33-1	£1.29	30-1	£1.41	£13.43
16-1	£4.31	20-1	£3.49	25-1	£1.67	33-1	£1.28	35-1	£1.21	£13.16
16-1	£4.30	20-1	£3.48	25-1	£1.66	33-1	£1.27	40-1	£1.06	£12.95

Note: total outlay = stakes plus tax.

7

THE PROFIT TARGET METHOD

SIX AGAINST THE FIELD

Method 1: Stake on all six selections so that if any one of the six is the winner you recoup the total outlay and make a predetermined profit.

SIX AGAINST THE FIELD
(Profit Target £20)

Runners	Odds	Stake	Return	Profit
A	10-1	£2.92	£32.12	£20.01
B	15-1	£2.01	£32.16	£20.05
C	16-1	£1.90	£32.30	£20.19
D	20-1	£1.54	£32.34	£20.23
E	22-1	£1.40	£32.20	£20.09
F	25-1	£1.24	£32.24	£20.13
	Stakes	£11.01		
	Tax	£1.10		
	Total outlay	£12.11		

Total outlay £12.11.
If any one of the six selections is the winner, net profit £20.

SIX AGAINST THE FIELD
(Profit Target £20)

Odds	Stake	Odds	Stake	Odds	Stake	Odds	Stake	Odds	Stake	Odds	Stake	Total Outlay
20-1	£1.53	10-1	£2.92	25-1	£1.24	15-1	£2.01	15-1	£2.01	25-1	£1.24	£12.04
20-1	£1.52	10-1	£2.89	25-1	£1.23	15-1	£1.99	15-1	£1.99	30-1	£1.03	£11.71
20-1	£1.50	10-1	£2.86	25-1	£1.22	15-1	£1.97	15-1	£1.97	35-1	£0.88	£11.44
20-1	£1.50	10-1	£2.85	25-1	£1.21	15-1	£1.96	15-1	£1.96	40-1	£0.77	£11.28
10-1	£2.92	15-1	£2.01	16-1	£1.90	20-1	£1.54	22-1	£1.40	25-1	£1.24	£12.11
10-1	£2.89	15-1	£1.99	16-1	£1.87	20-1	£1.52	22-1	£1.39	30-1	£1.03	£11.76
10-1	£2.87	15-1	£1.98	16-1	£1.86	20-1	£1.51	22-1	£1.38	35-1	£0.88	£11.53
10-1	£2.85	15-1	£1.96	16-1	£1.85	20-1	£1.50	22-1	£1.37	40-1	£0.77	£11.33
10-1	£2.79	15-1	£1.92	20-1	£1.47	22-1	£1.34	25-1	£1.19	30-1	£1.00	£10.68
10-1	£2.77	15-1	£1.91	20-1	£1.46	22-1	£1.33	25-1	£1.18	35-1	£0.85	£10.45
10-1	£2.76	15-1	£1.90	20-1	£1.45	22-1	£1.32	25-1	£1.17	40-1	£0.75	£10.28
10-1	£3.11	12-1	£2.63	15-1	£2.14	16-1	£2.01	20-1	£1.63	25-1	£1.32	£14.12
10-1	£3.07	12-1	£2.60	15-1	£2.11	16-1	£1.99	20-1	£1.61	30-1	£1.10	£13.73
10-1	£3.05	12-1	£2.58	15-1	£2.10	16-1	£1.97	20-1	£1.60	35-1	£0.94	£13.46
10-1	£3.03	12-1	£2.56	15-1	£2.08	16-1	£1.96	20-1	£1.59	40-1	£0.82	£13.24

Note: total outlay = stakes plus tax.

Method 2: Take three runners to be the banker team to make a set profit and then stake on the other three selections to show a smaller profit.

SIX AGAINST THE FIELD
(Team A/B/C Profit Target £40)
(Team D/E/F Profit Target £20)

Runners	Odds	Stake	Return	Profit
A	20-1	£2.76	£57.96	£40.13
B	10-1	£5.26	£57.86	£40.03
C	15-1	£3.62	£57.92	£40.09

D	22-1	£1.65	£37.95	£20.12
E	25-1	£1.46	£37.96	£20.13
F	25-1	£1.46	£37.96	£20.13
	Stakes	£16.21		
	Tax	£1.62		
	Total outlay	£17.83		

Total outlay £17.83.

If Runner A, B or C is the winner, net profit £40.
If Runner D, E or F is the winner, net profit £20.

SIX AGAINST THE FIELD
(Team A/B/C Profit Target £40)
(Team D/E/F Profit Target £20)

Odds	Stake	Odds	Stake	Odds	Stake	Odds	Stake	Odds	Stake	Odds	Stake	Total Outlay
15-1	£3.61	16-1	£3.40	20-1	£2.76	10-1	£3.43	25-1	£1.46	25-1	£1.46	£17.73
15-1	£3.59	16-1	£3.38	20-1	£2.74	10-1	£3.40	25-1	£1.44	30-1	£1.21	£17.34
15-1	£3.57	16-1	£3.36	20-1	£2.72	10-1	£3.37	25-1	£1.43	35-1	£1.04	£17.04
15-1	£3.56	16-1	£3.35	20-1	£2.71	10-1	£3.35	25-1	£1.42	40-1	£0.91	£16.83
10-1	£5.33	20-1	£2.80	25-1	£2.26	15-1	£2.42	16-1	£2.28	20-1	£1.85	£18.63
10-1	£5.28	20-1	£2.77	25-1	£2.24	15-1	£2.38	16-1	£2.24	25-1	£1.47	£18.02
10-1	£5.24	20-1	£2.75	25-1	£2.22	15-1	£2.36	16-1	£2.22	30-1	£1.22	£17.61
10-1	£5.22	20-1	£2.74	25-1	£2.21	15-1	£2.34	16-1	£2.20	35-1	£1.04	£17.33
25-1	£2.19	10-1	£5.17	15-1	£3.56	20-1	£1.76	25-1	£1.42	30-1	£1.20	£16.83
25-1	£2.18	10-1	£5.15	15-1	£3.54	20-1	£1.75	25-1	£1.41	35-1	£1.02	£16.56
25-1	£2.18	10-1	£5.13	15-1	£3.53	20-1	£1.74	25-1	£1.41	40-1	£0.90	£16.38
15-1	£3.53	20-1	£2.69	25-1	£2.17	10-1	£3.31	20-1	£1.74	25-1	£1.40	£16.32
15-1	£3.50	20-1	£2.67	25-1	£2.16	10-1	£3.27	20-1	£1.72	30-1	£1.17	£15.94
15-1	£3.48	20-1	£2.66	25-1	£2.15	10-1	£3.25	20-1	£1.71	35-1	£1.00	£15.68
15-1	£3.47	20-1	£2.65	25-1	£2.14	10-1	£3.23	20-1	£1.70	40-1	£0.87	£15.47

Note: total outlay = stakes plus tax.

SIX AGAINST THE FIELD
(Team A/B/C Profit Target £50)
(Team D/E/F Profit Target £25)

Odds	Stake	Odds	Stake	Odds	Stake	Odds	Stake	Odds	Stake	Odds	Stake	Total Outlay
10-1	£6.68	15-1	£4.59	20-1	£3.50	20-1	£2.31	20-1	£2.31	25-1	£1.87	£23.39
10-1	£6.63	15-1	£4.56	20-1	£3.48	20-1	£2.29	20-1	£2.29	30-1	£1.55	£22.88
10-1	£6.60	15-1	£4.54	20-1	£3.46	20-1	£2.27	20-1	£2.27	35-1	£1.33	£22.52
10-1	£6.57	15-1	£4.52	20-1	£3.45	20-1	£2.26	20-1	£2.26	40-1	£1.16	£22.24
10-1	£6.61	15-1	£4.55	20-1	£3.47	20-1	£2.27	25-1	£1.84	25-1	£1.84	£22.64
10-1	£6.56	15-1	£4.51	20-1	£3.44	20-1	£2.25	25-1	£1.82	30-1	£1.53	£22.12
10-1	£6.53	15-1	£4.49	20-1	£3.42	20-1	£2.23	25-1	£1.81	35-1	£1.31	£21.77
15-1	£4.38	15-1	£4.38	20-1	£3.34	20-1	£2.15	20-1	£2.15	25-1	£1.74	£19.95
15-1	£4.35	15-1	£4.35	20-1	£3.32	20-1	£2.12	20-1	£2.12	30-1	£1.44	£19.47
15-1	£4.33	15-1	£4.33	20-1	£3.30	20-1	£2.11	20-1	£2.11	35-1	£1.23	£19.15
15-1	£4.23	20-1	£3.23	20-1	£3.23	20-1	£2.04	25-1	£1.65	25-1	£1.65	£17.63
15-1	£4.21	20-1	£3.21	20-1	£3.21	20-1	£2.02	25-1	£1.63	30-1	£1.37	£17.22
15-1	£4.19	20-1	£3.19	20-1	£3.19	20-1	£2.00	25-1	£1.62	35-1	£1.17	£16.90
20-1	£3.09	20-1	£3.09	22-1	£2.82	25-1	£1.53	25-1	£1.53	30-1	£1.29	£14.69
20-1	£3.07	20-1	£3.07	22-1	£2.81	25-1	£1.52	25-1	£1.52	35-1	£1.10	£14.40
20-1	£3.06	20-1	£3.06	22-1	£2.80	25-1	£1.52	25-1	£1.52	40-1	£0.96	£14.21

Note: total outlay = stakes plus tax.

THE EASY
POCKET
CALCULATOR
METHOD

8

THE SET AMOUNT METHOD

Two Against The Field

Not everyone is computer-minded or even has access to a computer, but the formula can in fact be applied in a very straightforward way with a pocket calculator or even using pen and paper by means of the SET AMOUNT method.

In this version of the formula the backer determines the outlay rather than the profit target as the first stage in framing a bet. Calculations are much less complex, and even for the computer fan this may be the preferred approach.

Also the set amount method can be adapted for betting tax quite simply by adding the percentage onto total outlay, without incorporating tax into the calculations, as in the most complete application of the formula. In this way the backer still eliminates the higher deduction on the return and in the long run will gain on a winning run.

In every way, therefore, this method is a viable alternative for the backer who is not using a computer.

The idea is to stake a set amount on two runners or more. Let's take an example. Say you have £5 to lay out and your two selections are A 2-1 and B 6-1.

Here's your systematic wager:

Runners	Odds	Stake	Return	Profit
A	2-1	£3.50	£10.50	£5.50
B	6-1	£1.50	£10.50	£5.50
		£5.00		

Your set amount of £5 has been *proportioned* between your two selections and if either is the winner the return will be £10.50 which includes your £5 outlay, so your net profit is £5.50.

You can apply the same systematic approach to ante post races. Here's an example. In September 1988 the ante post odds for the following year's Epsom Derby were 12-1 against High Estate and 20-1 Nashwan. With a set outlay of £10 here is the systematic wager:

Runners	Odds	Stake	Return	Profit
A	12-1	£6.18	£80.34	£70.34
B	20-1	£3.88	£80.22	£70.22
		£10.00		

The Set Amount Formula

Call your two selections Runner A and Runner B.

Stake for Runner A is **B+1** x £? divided by A+B+2.
Stake for Runner B is **A+1** x £? divided by A+B+2.

Where you see the question mark insert the set amount you require. Say you have £5 to invest in your two selections at odds of A 2-1 and B 6-1.

Stake A 6+1 x £5 = 35 divided by 2+6+2 = 10 which is 35 divided by 10 = £3.50.
Stake B 2+1 x £5 = 15 divided by 10 = £1.50.

So your £5 has been proportioned as to £3.50 on Runner A and £1.50 on Runner B. If either A or B wins the return will be £10.50. So we have recouped the total stakes and made a net profit of £5.50.

Let's work the formula with ante post odds of A 12-1 and B 15-1 and assume that we have £10 to lay out.

Stake A 15+1 x £10 divided by 12+15+2. Stake for A is 160 divided by 29 = £5.52.
Stake B 12+1 x £10 divided by 12+15+2. Stake for B is 130 divided by 29 = £4.48.

Runners	Odds	Stake	Return	Profit
A	12-1	£5.52	£71.76	£61.76
B	15-1	£4.48	£71.68	£61.68
		£10.00		

Now that you have the formula you can compile your own staking tables, but to save you a certain amount of effort the following tables cover many of the most common prices and will help you start to use the set amount method as an aid to profitable betting.

TWO AGAINST THE FIELD
(Total Outlay is STAKES + TAX = £2)

Odds	Stake	Return	Odds	Stake	Return
2-1	£1.04	£3.12	3-1	£0.78	£3.12
2-1	£1.14	£3.42	4-1	£0.68	£3.40
2-1	£1.21	£3.63	5-1	£0.61	£3.66
2-1	£1.27	£3.81	6-1	£0.55	£3.85
2-1	£1.32	£3.96	7-1	£0.50	£4.00
2-1	£1.37	£4.11	8-1	£0.46	£4.14
2-1	£1.40	£4.20	9-1	£0.42	£4.20
2-1	£1.43	£4.29	10-1	£0.39	£4.29

TWO AGAINST THE FIELD
(Total Outlay is STAKES + TAX = £2)

Odds	Stake	Return	Odds	Stake	Return
3-1	£1.01	£4.04	4-1	£0.81	£4.05
3-1	£1.09	£4.36	5-1	£0.73	£4.38
3-1	£1.16	£4.64	6-1	£0.66	£4.62
3-1	£1.21	£4.84	7-1	£0.61	£4.88
3-1	£1.26	£5.04	8-1	£0.56	£5.04
3-1	£1.30	£5.20	9-1	£0.52	£5.20
3-1	£1.33	£5.32	10-1	£0.49	£5.39
4-1	£0.99	£4.95	5-1	£0.83	£4.98
4-1	£1.06	£5.30	6-1	£0.76	£5.32
4-1	£1.12	£5.60	7-1	£0.70	£5.60
4-1	£1.17	£5.85	8-1	£0.65	£5.85
4-1	£1.21	£6.05	9-1	£0.61	£6.10
4-1	£1.25	£6.25	10-1	£0.57	£6.27
5-1	£0.98	£5.88	6-1	£0.84	£5.88
5-1	£1.04	£6.24	7-1	£0.78	£6.24
5-1	£1.09	£6.54	8-1	£0.73	£6.57
5-1	£1.14	£6.84	9-1	£0.68	£6.80
5-1	£1.18	£7.08	10-1	£0.64	£7.04
6-1	£0.97	£6.79	7-1	£0.85	£6.80
6-1	£1.02	£7.14	8-1	£0.80	£7.20
6-1	£1.07	£7.49	9-1	£0.75	£7.50
6-1	£1.11	£7.77	10-1	£0.71	£7.81
7-1	£0.96	£7.68	8-1	£0.86	£7.74
7-1	£1.01	£8.08	9-1	£0.81	£8.10
7-1	£1.05	£8.40	10-1	£0.77	£8.47
8-1	£0.96	£8.64	9-1	£0.86	£8.60
8-1	£1.00	£9.00	10-1	£0.82	£9.02
8-1	£1.04	£9.36	11-1	£0.78	£9.36
9-1	£0.95	£9.50	10-1	£0.87	£9.57
9-1	£0.99	£9.90	11-1	£0.83	£9.96

TWO AGAINST THE FIELD
(Total Outlay is STAKES + TAX = £3)

Odds	Stake	Return	Odds	Stake	Return
2-1	£1.56	£4.68	3-1	£1.17	£4.68
2-1	£1.71	£5.13	4-1	£1.02	£5.10
2-1	£1.82	£5.46	5-1	£0.91	£5.46
2-1	£1.91	£5.73	6-1	£0.82	£5.74
2-1	£1.99	£5.97	7-1	£0.74	£5.92
2-1	£2.05	£6.15	8-1	£0.68	£6.12
2-1	£2.10	£6.30	9-1	£0.63	£6.30
2-1	£2.15	£6.45	10-1	£0.59	£6.49
3-1	£1.52	£6.08	4-1	£1.21	£6.05
3-1	£1.64	£6.56	5-1	£1.09	£6.54
3-1	£1.74	£6.96	6-1	£0.99	£6.93
3-1	£1.82	£7.28	7-1	£0.91	£7.28
3-1	£1.89	£7.56	8-1	£0.84	£7.56
3-1	£1.95	£7.80	9-1	£0.78	£7.80
3-1	£2.00	£8.00	10-1	£0.73	£8.03
4-1	£1.49	£7.45	5-1	£1.24	£7.44
4-1	£1.59	£7.95	6-1	£1.14	£7.98
4-1	£1.68	£8.40	7-1	£1.05	£8.40
4-1	£1.76	£8.80	8-1	£0.98	£8.82
4-1	£1.82	£9.10	9-1	£0.91	£9.10
4-1	£1.88	£9.40	10-1	£0.85	£9.35
5-1	£1.47	£8.82	6-1	£1.26	£8.82
5-1	£1.56	£9.36	7-1	£1.17	£9.36
5-1	£1.64	£9.84	8-1	£1.09	£9.81
5-1	£1.71	£10.26	9-1	£1.02	£10.20
5-1	£1.77	£10.62	10-1	£0.96	£10.56
6-1	£1.46	£10.22	7-1	£1.27	£10.16
6-1	£1.54	£10.78	8-1	£1.19	£10.71
6-1	£1.61	£11.27	9-1	£1.12	£11.20
6-1	£1.67	£11.69	10-1	£1.06	£11.66

TWO AGAINST THE FIELD
(Total Outlay is STAKES + TAX = £3)

Odds	Stake	Return	Odds	Stake	Return
7-1	£1.45	£11.60	8-1	£1.28	£11.52
7-1	£1.52	£12.16	9-1	£1.21	£12.10
7-1	£1.58	£12.64	10-1	£1.15	£12.65
8-1	£1.44	£12.96	9-1	£1.29	£12.90
8-1	£1.50	£13.50	10-1	£1.23	£13.53
9-1	£1.43	£14.30	10-1	£1.30	£14.30
9-1	£1.49	£14.90	11-1	£1.24	£14.88

TWO AGAINST THE FIELD
(Total Outlay is STAKES + TAX = £4)

Odds	Stake	Return	Odds	Stake	Return
2-1	£2.08	£6.24	3-1	£1.56	£6.24
2-1	£2.27	£6.81	4-1	£1.37	£6.85
2-1	£2.43	£7.29	5-1	£1.21	£7.26
2-1	£2.55	£7.65	6-1	£1.09	£7.63
2-1	£2.65	£7.95	7-1	£0.99	£7.92
2-1	£2.73	£8.19	8-1	£0.91	£8.19
2-1	£2.80	£8.40	9-1	£0.84	£8.40
2-1	£2.86	£8.58	10-1	£0.78	£8.58
3-1	£2.02	£8.08	4-1	£1.62	£8.10
3-1	£2.18	£8.72	5-1	£1.46	£8.76
3-1	£2.32	£9.28	6-1	£1.32	£9.24
3-1	£2.43	£9.72	7-1	£1.21	£9.68
3-1	£2.52	£10.08	8-1	£1.12	£10.08
3-1	£2.60	£10.40	9-1	£1.04	£10.40
3-1	£2.67	£10.68	10-1	£0.97	£10.67

TWO AGAINST THE FIELD
(Total Outlay is STAKES + TAX = £4)

Odds	Stake	Return	Odds	Stake	Return
4-1	£1.99	£9.95	5-1	£1.65	£9.90
4-1	£2.12	£10.60	6-1	£1.52	£10.64
4-1	£2.24	£11.20	7-1	£1.40	£11.20
4-1	£2.34	£11.70	8-1	£1.30	£11.70
4-1	£2.43	£12.15	9-1	£1.21	£12.10
4-1	£2.50	£12.50	10-1	£1.14	£12.54
5-1	£1.96	£11.76	6-1	£1.68	£11.76
5-1	£2.08	£12.48	7-1	£1.56	£12.48
5-1	£2.18	£13.08	8-1	£1.46	£13.14
5-1	£2.27	£13.62	9-1	£1.37	£13.70
5-1	£2.36	£14.16	10-1	£1.28	£14.08
6-1	£1.94	£13.58	7-1	£1.70	£13.60
6-1	£2.05	£14.35	8-1	£1.59	£14.31
6-1	£2.14	£14.98	9-1	£1.50	£15.00
6-1	£2.22	£15.54	10-1	£1.42	£15.62
7-1	£1.93	£15.44	8-1	£1.71	£15.39
7-1	£2.02	£16.16	9-1	£1.62	£16.20
7-1	£2.11	£16.88	10-1	£1.53	£16.83
8-1	£1.92	£17.28	9-1	£1.72	£17.20
8-1	£2.00	£18.00	10-1	£1.64	£18.04
8-1	£2.08	£18.72	11-1	£1.56	£18.72
9-1	£1.91	£19.10	10-1	£1.73	£19.03
9-1	£1.99	£19.90	11-1	£1.65	£19.80

TWO AGAINST THE FIELD
(Total Outlay is STAKES + TAX = £5)

Odds	Stake	Return	Odds	Stake	Return
2-1	£2.60	£7.80	3-1	£1.95	£7.80
2-1	£2.84	£8.52	4-1	£1.71	£8.55
2-1	£3.03	£9.09	5-1	£1.52	£9.12
2-1	£3.19	£9.57	6-1	£1.37	£9.59
2-1	£3.31	£9.93	7-1	£1.24	£9.92
2-1	£3.41	£10.23	8-1	£1.14	£10.26
2-1	£3.50	£10.50	9-1	£1.05	£10.50
2-1	£3.58	£10.74	10-1	£0.98	£10.78
3-1	£2.53	£10.12	4-1	£2.02	£10.10
3-1	£2.73	£10.92	5-1	£1.82	£10.92
3-1	£2.90	£11.60	6-1	£1.65	£11.55
3-1	£3.03	£12.12	7-1	£1.52	£12.16
3-1	£3.15	£12.60	8-1	£1.40	£12.60
3-1	£3.25	£13.00	9-1	£1.30	£13.00
3-1	£3.34	£13.36	10-1	£1.21	£13.31
4-1	£2.48	£12.40	5-1	£2.07	£12.42
4-1	£2.65	£13.25	6-1	£1.90	£13.30
4-1	£2.80	£14.00	7-1	£1.75	£14.00
4-1	£2.93	£14.65	8-1	£1.63	£14.67
4-1	£3.03	£15.15	9-1	£1.52	£15.20
4-1	£3.13	£15.65	10-1	£1.42	£15.62
5-1	£2.45	£14.70	6-1	£2.10	£14.70
5-1	£2.60	£15.60	7-1	£1.95	£15.60
5-1	£2.73	£16.38	8-1	£1.82	£16.38
5-1	£2.84	£17.04	9-1	£1.71	£17.10
5-1	£2.94	£17.64	10-1	£1.61	£17.71
6-1	£2.43	£17.01	7-1	£2.12	£16.96
6-1	£2.56	£17.92	8-1	£1.99	£17.91
6-1	£2.68	£18.76	9-1	£1.87	£18.70
6-1	£2.78	£19.46	10-1	£1.77	£19.47

TWO AGAINST THE FIELD
(Total Outlay is STAKES + TAX = £5)

Odds	Stake	Return	Odds	Stake	Return
7-1	£2.41	£19.28	8-1	£2.14	£19.26
7-1	£2.53	£20.24	9-1	£2.02	£20.20
7-1	£2.63	£21.04	10-1	£1.92	£21.12
8-1	£2.39	£21.51	9-1	£2.16	£21.66
8-1	£2.50	£22.50	10-1	£2.05	£22.55
9-1	£2.38	£23.80	10-1	£2.17	£23.87
9-1	£2.48	£24.80	11-1	£2.07	£24.84

TWO AGAINST THE FIELD
(Total Outlay is STAKES + TAX = £6)

Double the £3.00 Staking Table

TWO AGAINST THE FIELD
(Total Outlay is STAKES + TAX = £7)

Odds	Stake	Return	Odds	Stake	Return
2-1	£3.63	£10.89	3-1	£2.73	£10.92
2-1	£3.98	£11.94	4-1	£2.39	£11.95
2-1	£4.24	£12.72	5-1	£2.12	£12.72
2-1	£4.45	£13.35	6-1	£1.91	£13.37
2-1	£4.63	£13.89	7-1	£1.73	£13.84
2-1	£4.77	£14.31	8-1	£1.59	£14.31
2-1	£4.89	£14.67	9-1	£1.47	£14.70
2-1	£5.00	£15.00	10-1	£1.36	£14.96

TWO AGAINST THE FIELD
(Total Outlay is STAKES + TAX = £7)

Odds	Stake	Return	Odds	Stake	Return
3-1	£3.53	£14.12	4-1	£2.83	£14.15
3-1	£3.82	£15.28	5-1	£2.54	£15.24
3-1	£4.05	£16.20	6-1	£2.31	£16.17
3-1	£4.24	£16.96	7-1	£2.12	£16.96
3-1	£4.40	£17.60	8-1	£1.96	£17.64
3-1	£4.54	£18.16	9-1	£1.82	£18.20
3-1	£4.66	£18.64	10-1	£1.70	£18.70
4-1	£3.47	£17.35	5-1	£2.89	£17.43
4-1	£3.71	£18.55	6-1	£2.65	£18.55
4-1	£3.91	£19.55	7-1	£2.45	£19.60
4-1	£4.09	£20.45	8-1	£2.27	£20.43
4-1	£4.24	£21.20	9-1	£2.12	£21.20
4-1	£4.37	£21.85	10-1	£1.99	£21.89
5-1	£3.42	£20.52	6-1	£2.94	£20.58
5-1	£3.63	£21.78	7-1	£2.73	£21.84
5-1	£3.82	£22.92	8-1	£2.54	£22.86
5-1	£3.98	£23.88	9-1	£2.39	£23.90
5-1	£4.12	£24.72	10-1	£2.24	£24.64
6-1	£3.39	£23.73	7-1	£2.97	£23.76
6-1	£3.58	£25.06	8-1	£2.78	£25.02
6-1	£3.74	£26.18	9-1	£2.62	£26.20
6-1	£3.89	£27.23	10-1	£2.47	£27.17
7-1	£3.37	£26.96	8-1	£2.99	£26.91
7-1	£3.53	£28.24	9-1	£2.83	£28.30
7-1	£3.68	£29.44	10-1	£2.68	£29.48
8-1	£3.35	£30.15	9-1	£3.01	£30.10
8-1	£3.50	£31.50	10-1	£2.86	£31.46
9-1	£3.33	£33.30	10-1	£3.03	£33.33
9-1	£3.47	£34.70	11-1	£2.89	£34.68

TWO AGAINST THE FIELD
(Total Outlay is STAKES + TAX = £8)

Double the £4.00 Staking Table

TWO AGAINST THE FIELD
(Total Outlay is STAKES + TAX = £9)

Odds	Stake	Return	Odds	Stake	Return
2-1	£4.67	£14.01	3-1	£3.51	£14.04
2-1	£5.11	£15.33	4-1	£3.07	£15.35
2-1	£5.45	£16.35	5-1	£2.73	£16.38
2-1	£5.73	£17.19	6-1	£2.45	£17.15
2-1	£5.95	£17.85	7-1	£2.23	£17.84
2-1	£6.14	£18.42	8-1	£2.05	£18.45
2-1	£6.29	£18.87	9-1	£1.89	£18.90
2-1	£6.43	£19.29	10-1	£1.75	£19.25
3-1	£4.54	£18.16	4-1	£3.64	£18.20
3-1	£4.91	£19.64	5-1	£3.27	£19.62
3-1	£5.21	£20.84	6-1	£2.97	£20.79
3-1	£5.45	£21.80	7-1	£2.73	£21.84
3-1	£5.66	£22.64	8-1	£2.52	£22.68
3-1	£5.84	£23.36	9-1	£2.34	£23.40
3-1	£6.00	£24.00	10-1	£2.18	£23.98
4-1	£4.46	£22.30	5-1	£3.72	£22.32
4-1	£4.77	£23.85	6-1	£3.41	£23.87
4-1	£5.03	£25.15	7-1	£3.15	£25.20
4-1	£5.26	£26.30	8-1	£2.92	£26.28
4-1	£5.45	£27.25	9-1	£2.73	£27.30
4-1	£5.62	£28.10	10-1	£2.56	£28.16

TWO AGAINST THE FIELD
(Total Outlay is STAKES + TAX = £9)

Odds	Stake	Return	Odds	Stake	Return
5-1	£4.40	£26.40	6-1	£3.78	£26.46
5-1	£4.67	£28.02	7-1	£3.51	£28.08
5-1	£4.91	£29.46	8-1	£3.27	£29.43
5-1	£5.11	£30.66	9-1	£3.07	£30.70
5-1	£5.29	£31.74	10-1	£2.89	£31.79
6-1	£4.36	£30.52	7-1	£3.82	£30.56
6-1	£4.60	£32.20	8-1	£3.58	£32.22
6-1	£4.81	£33.67	9-1	£3.37	£33.70
6-1	£5.00	£35.00	10-1	£3.18	£34.98
7-1	£4.33	£34.64	8-1	£3.85	£34.65
7-1	£4.54	£36.32	9-1	£3.64	£36.40
7-1	£4.74	£37.92	10-1	£3.44	£37.84
8-1	£4.31	£38.79	9-1	£3.87	£38.70
8-1	£4.50	£40.50	10-1	£3.68	£40.48
9-1	£4.28	£42.80	10-1	£3.90	£42.90
9-1	£4.46	£44.60	11-1	£3.72	£44.64

TWO AGAINST THE FIELD
(Total Outlay is STAKES + TAX = £10)

Odds	Stake	Return	Odds	Stake	Return
2-1	£5.19	£15.57	3-1	£3.90	£15.60
2-1	£5.68	£17.04	4-1	£3.41	£17.05
2-1	£6.06	£18.18	5-1	£3.03	£18.18
2-1	£6.36	£19.08	6-1	£2.73	£19.11
2-1	£6.61	£19.83	7-1	£2.48	£19.84
2-1	£6.82	£20.46	8-1	£2.27	£20.43
2-1	£6.99	£20.97	9-1	£2.10	£21.00
2-1	£7.14	£21.42	10-1	£1.95	£21.45

TWO AGAINST THE FIELD
(Total Outlay is STAKES + TAX = £10)

Odds	Stake	Return	Odds	Stake	Return
3-1	£5.05	£20.20	4-1	£4.04	£20.20
3-1	£5.45	£21.80	5-1	£3.64	£21.84
3-1	£5.78	£23.12	6-1	£3.31	£23.17
3-1	£6.06	£24.24	7-1	£3.03	£24.24
3-1	£6.29	£25.16	8-1	£2.80	£25.20
3-1	£6.49	£25.96	9-1	£2.60	£26.00
3-1	£6.67	£26.68	10-1	£2.42	£26.62
4-1	£4.96	£24.80	5-1	£4.13	£24.78
4-1	£5.30	£26.50	6-1	£3.79	£26.53
4-1	£5.59	£27.95	7-1	£3.50	£28.00
4-1	£5.84	£29.20	8-1	£3.25	£29.25
4-1	£6.06	£30.30	9-1	£3.03	£30.30
4-1	£6.25	£31.25	10-1	£2.84	£31.24
5-1	£4.89	£29.34	6-1	£4.20	£29.40
5-1	£5.19	£31.14	7-1	£3.90	£31.20
5-1	£5.45	£32.70	8-1	£3.64	£32.76
5-1	£5.68	£34.08	9-1	£3.41	£34.10
5-1	£5.88	£35.28	10-1	£3.21	£35.31
6-1	£4.85	£33.95	7-1	£4.24	£33.92
6-1	£5.11	£35.77	8-1	£3.98	£35.82
6-1	£5.35	£37.45	9-1	£3.74	£37.40
6-1	£5.56	£38.92	10-1	£3.54	£38.94
7-1	£4.81	£38.48	8-1	£4.28	£38.52
7-1	£5.05	£40.40	9-1	£4.40	£40.40
7-1	£5.26	£42.08	10-1	£3.83	£42.13
8-1	£4.78	£43.02	9-1	£4.31	£43.10
8-1	£5.00	£45.00	10-1	£4.09	£44.99
9-1	£4.76	£47.60	10-1	£4.33	£47.63
9-1	£4.96	£49.60	11-1	£4.13	£49.56

I hope that by now you will have worked thorough my basic Formula for *Two Against The Field — Set Amount*. If you have then you will be more comfortable in "reading" this more sophisticated version, which turns out the fully calculated bet, with *Tax Paid On*. You don't have to study it of course because the staking tables will meet most of your betting needs, but as I have suggested before, you will be in a much stronger winning position if you can figure out how the principles work. And that is my objective.

Here this is the setting for a successful bet based on Two Against the Field — Tax Paid On — Limit £10.00.

THE EXAMPLE BET

$$\text{Runner A at } 3\text{-}1$$
$$\text{Runner B at } 4\text{-}1$$

Set Limit   £10

ELEMENTS OF THE FORMULA

$$\text{Set Limit} = \mathbf{L}$$
$$\text{Total Stake: } \pounds\text{'s bet} = \mathbf{Ts}$$
$$\text{Tax (at 10\% of } \pounds\text{'s bet)} = \mathbf{Tx}$$

$$\text{Runner A odds (3-1)} = \mathbf{A}$$
$$\text{Runner B odds (4-1)} = \mathbf{B}$$

$$
\begin{aligned}
\text{Total stake } (\mathbf{Ts}) &= ([L \times 100]) \div 110 \\
&= ([\pounds10 \times 100]) \div 110 \\
&= \pounds9.09
\end{aligned}
$$

$$
\begin{aligned}
\text{Tax at 10\% } (\mathbf{Tx}) &= (L - Ts) \\
&= (\pounds10 - 9.09) \\
&= 91p
\end{aligned}
$$

$$
\begin{aligned}
\text{Stake Runner A: } (B+1) &= \mathbf{S1} \\
(4+1) &= \mathbf{S1} \\
5 &= \mathbf{S1}
\end{aligned}
$$

Stake Runner **B**: (A+1) = **S2**
$$(3+1) = \textbf{S2}$$
$$4 = \textbf{S2}$$

A+B in Combination = **S3**
$$\textbf{S1} + \textbf{S2} = \textbf{S3}$$
$$5 + 4 = \textbf{S3}$$

FORMULAE

Runner **A**: Stake = ([**S1**] × [**TS**]) ÷ S3 = **As**
$$([4{+}1] \times £9.09) \div 9 = \textbf{As}$$
$$5 \times £9.09 \div 9 = £5.05$$
$$\textbf{AS} = £5.05$$

Runner **B**: Stake = ([**S2**] × [**TS**]) ÷ S3 = **Bs**
$$([4] \times £9.09) \div 9 = \textbf{Bs}$$
$$4 \times £9.09 \div 9 = £4.04$$
$$\textbf{AS} = £4.04$$

Runners	Odds	Stake	Return	Profit
A	3-1	£5.05	£20.20	£10.20
B	4-1	£4.04	£20.20	£10.20
	Total	£9.09		
	Tax	.91		
	Outlay	£10.00		

Total stake £9.09 plus tax at 10%, 91p equals £10.

If runner A or B wins the RETURN will be £20.20. Deduct your outlay to win a Net Profit of £10.20.

TWO AGAINST THE FIELD
(Total Outlay is STAKES + TAX = £10)

Odds	Stake	Return	Odds	Stake	Return
3-1	£5.05	£20.20	4-1	£4.04	£20.20
3-1	£5.45	£21.80	5-1	£3.64	£21.84
3-1	£5.78	£23.12	6-1	£3.31	£23.17
3-1	£6.06	£24.24	7-1	£3.03	£24.24
3-1	£6.29	£25.16	8-1	£2.80	£25.20
4-1	£4.96	£24.80	5-1	£4.13	£24.78
4-1	£5.30	£26.50	6-1	£3.79	£26.53
4-1	£5.59	£27.95	7-1	£3.50	£28.00
4-1	£5.84	£29.20	8-1	£3.25	£29.25
5-1	£4.89	£29.34	6-1	£4.20	£29.40
5-1	£5.19	£31.14	7-1	£3.90	£31.20
5-1	£5.45	£32.70	8-1	£3.64	£32.76
5-1	£5.68	£34.08	9-1	£3.41	£34.10
6-1	£4.85	£33.95	7-1	£4.24	£33.92
6-1	£5.11	£35.77	8-1	£3.98	£35.82
6-1	£5.35	£37.45	9-1	£3.74	£37.40
6-1	£5.56	£38.92	10-1	£3.54	£38.94
7-1	£4.81	£38.48	8-1	£4.28	£38.52
7-1	£5.05	£40.40	9-1	£4.40	£40.40
7-1	£5.26	£42.08	10-1	£3.83	£42.13

TWO AGAINST THE FIELD
(Total Outlay is STAKES + TAX = £20)

Odds	Stake	Return	Odds	Stake	Return
10-1	£10.77	£118.47	15-1	£7.41	£118.56
10-1	£11.93	£131.23	20-1	£6.25	£131.25
10-1	£12.78	£140.58	25-1	£5.40	£140.40
10-1	£13.42	£147.62	30-1	£4.76	£147.56
15-1	£10.32	£165.12	20-1	£7.86	£165.06
15-1	£11.25	£180.00	25-1	£6.93	£180.18
15-1	£11.99	£191.84	30-1	£6.19	£191.89
15-1	£12.59	£201.44	35-1	£5.59	£201.24
20-1	£10.06	£211.26	25-1	£8.12	£211.12
20-1	£10.84	£227.64	30-1	£7.34	£227.54
20-1	£11.48	£241.08	35-1	£6.70	£241.20
22-1	£9.65	£211.95	25-1	£8.53	£221.78
22-1	£10.44	£240.12	30-1	£7.74	£239.94
22-1	£11.09	£255.07	35-1	£7.09	£255.24
22-1	£11.65	£267.95	40-1	£6.53	£267.73
25-1	£9.09	£236.34	25-1	£9.09	£236.34
25-1	£9.89	£257.14	30-1	£8.29	£256.99
25-1	£10.56	£274.56	35-1	£7.62	£274.32

9

THE SET AMOUNT METHOD

THREE PLUS AGAINST THE FIELD

When you have a fixed amount to lay out on three runners in the same race you can again operate the set amount method to arrive at the correct stakes for each. Have a look at this example:

Runner A 8-1, Runner B 10-1 and Runner C 15-1. Total Limit £10.

THREE AGAINST THE FIELD
(Outlay £10)

Runners	Odds	Stake	Return	Profit
A	8-1	£4.20	£37.80	£27.80
B	10-1	£3.44	£37.84	£27.84
C	15-1	£2.36	£37.76	£27.76
		£10.00		

Total stakes available = £10.

If any one of your three selections is the winner you make the same amount of profit.

Three Against — The Formula

Stake for **A** is S = B+1 x C+1.
Stake for **B** is S1 = A+1 x C+1.
Stake for **C** is S2 = A+1 x B+1.
            T = S + S1 + S2.
S3 = S x £10 divided by T.
S4 = S1 x £10 divided by T.
S5 = S2 x £10 divided by T.

Let's apply the formula with our example of **A** 8-1, **B** 10-1 and **C** 15-1. Outlay £10.

S = 11 x 16 = 176.
S1 = 9 x 16 = 144.
S2 = 9 x 11 = 99.
T = 176 + 144 + 99 = 419.
S3 = 176 x £10 = 1760 divided by 419 = £4.20 stake A.
S4 = 144 x £10 = 1440 divided by 419 = £3.44 stake B.
S5 = 99 x £10 = 990 divided by 419 = £2.36 stake C.

When you have the time to spare you can compile your own staking tables covering the most likely amounts of your outlay. But to save you a lot of arithmetic I have compiled some tables on the computer. All you have to do is to refer to the table which covers your outlay.

THREE AGAINST THE FIELD
(Outlay £5)

Odds	Stake	Odds	Stake	Odds	Stake
2-1	£2.13	3-1	£1.60	4-1	£1.28
2-1	£2.22	3-1	£1.67	5-1	£1.11
2-1	£2.30	3-1	£1.72	6-1	£0.98
2-1	£2.35	3-1	£1.76	7-1	£0.88
2-1	£2.40	3-1	£1.80	8-1	£0.80
2-1	£2.44	3-1	£1.83	9-1	£0.73
2-1	£2.47	3-1	£1.85	10-1	£0.67

THREE AGAINST THE FIELD
(Outlay £5)

Odds	Stake	Odds	Stake	Odds	Stake
2-1	£2.38	4-1	£1.43	5-1	£1.19
2-1	£2.46	4-1	£1.48	6-1	£1.06
2-1	£2.53	4-1	£1.52	7-1	£0.95
2-1	£2.59	4-1	£1.55	8-1	£0.86
2-1	£2.63	4-1	£1.58	9-1	£0.79
2-1	£2.67	4-1	£1.60	10-1	£0.73
3-1	£2.03	4-1	£1.62	5-1	£1.35
3-1	£2.11	4-1	£1.69	6-1	£1.20
3-1	£2.17	4-1	£1.74	7-1	£1.09
3-1	£2.23	4-1	£1.78	8-1	£0.99
3-1	£2.27	4-1	£1.82	9-1	£0.91
3-1	£2.31	4-1	£1.85	10-1	£0.84
3-1	£2.23	5-1	£1.49	6-1	£1.28
3-1	£2.31	5-1	£1.54	7-1	£1.15
3-1	£2.37	5-1	£1.58	8-1	£1.05
3-1	£2.42	5-1	£1.61	9-1	£0.97
3-1	£2.46	5-1	£1.64	10-1	£0.90
4-1	£1.96	5-1	£1.64	6-1	£1.40
4-1	£2.03	5-1	£1.69	7-1	£1.27
4-1	£2.09	5-1	£1.74	8-1	£1.16
4-1	£2.14	5-1	£1.79	9-1	£1.07
4-1	£2.19	5-1	£1.82	10-1	£0.99
5-1	£1.75	6-1	£1.50	7-1	£1.31
5-1	£1.80	6-1	£1.55	8-1	£1.20
5-1	£1.85	6-1	£1.59	9-1	£1.11
6-1	£1.72	7-1	£1.50	8-1	£1.33
6-1	£1.77	7-1	£1.55	9-1	£1.24
6-1	£1.81	7-1	£1.59	10-1	£1.15

THREE AGAINST THE FIELD
(Outlay £8)

Odds	Stake	Odds	Stake	Odds	Stake
3-1	£3.24	4-1	£2.59	5-1	£2.16
3-1	£3.37	4-1	£2.70	6-1	£1.93
3-1	£3.48	4-1	£2.78	7-1	£1.74
3-1	£3.56	4-1	£2.85	8-1	£1.58
3-1	£3.64	4-1	£2.91	9-1	£1.45
3-1	£3.70	4-1	£2.96	10-1	£1.34
3-1	£3.57	5-1	£2.38	6-1	£2.04
3-1	£3.69	5-1	£2.46	7-1	£1.85
3-1	£3.79	5-1	£2.53	8-1	£1.68
3-1	£3.87	5-1	£2.58	9-1	£1.55
3-1	£3.94	5-1	£2.63	10-1	£1.43
4-1	£3.14	5-1	£2.62	6-1	£2.24
4-1	£3.25	5-1	£2.71	7-1	£2.03
4-1	£3.35	5-1	£2.79	8-1	£1.86
4-1	£3.43	5-1	£2.86	9-1	£1.71
4-1	£3.50	5-1	£2.91	10-1	£1.59
5-1	£3.07	6-1	£2.63	7-1	£2.30
5-1	£3.17	6-1	£2.72	8-1	£2.11
5-1	£3.26	6-1	£2.79	9-1	£1.95
5-1	£3.33	6-1	£2.85	10-1	£1.82
5-1	£3.31	7-1	£2.48	8-1	£2.21
5-1	£3.40	7-1	£2.55	9-1	£2.04
5-1	£3.49	7-1	£2.61	10-1	£1.90

THREE AGAINST THE FIELD
(Outlay £10)

Odds	Stake	Odds	Stake	Odds	Stake
2-1	£4.26	3-1	£3.19	4-1	£2.55
2-1	£4.44	3-1	£3.33	5-1	£2.22
2-1	£4.59	3-1	£3.44	6-1	£1.97
2-1	£4.71	3-1	£3.53	7-1	£1.76
2-1	£4.80	3-1	£3.60	8-1	£1.60
2-1	£4.88	3-1	£3.66	9-1	£1.46
2-1	£4.94	3-1	£3.71	10-1	£1.35
3-1	£4.05	4-1	£3.24	5-1	£2.70
3-1	£4.22	4-1	£3.37	6-1	£2.41
3-1	£4.35	4-1	£3.48	7-1	£2.17
3-1	£4.46	4-1	£3.56	8-1	£1.98
3-1	£4.55	4-1	£3.64	9-1	£1.82
3-1	£4.62	4-1	£3.70	10-1	£1.68
3-1	£4.47	5-1	£2.98	6-1	£2.55
3-1	£4.62	5-1	£3.08	7-1	£2.31
3-1	£4.74	5-1	£3.16	8-1	£2.11
3-1	£4.81	5-1	£3.23	9-1	£1.94
3-1	£4.93	5-1	£3.28	10-1	£1.79
4-1	£3.93	5-1	£3.27	6-1	£2.80
4-1	£4.07	5-1	£3.39	7-1	£2.54
4-1	£4.19	5-1	£3.49	8-1	£2.33
4-1	£4.29	5-1	£3.57	9-1	£2.14
4-1	£4.37	5-1	£3.64	10-1	£1.99
5-1	£3.84	6-1	£3.29	7-1	£2.88
5-1	£3.96	6-1	£3.40	8-1	£2.64
5-1	£4.07	6-1	£3.49	9-1	£2.44
5-1	£4.16	6-1	£3.57	10-1	£2.27

THREE AGAINST THE FIELD
(Ante Post Outlay £10)

Odds	Stake	Odds	Stake	Odds	Stake
8-1	£4.20	10-1	£3.44	15-1	£2.36
8-1	£4.45	10-1	£3.64	20-1	£1.91
8-1	£4.62	10-1	£3.78	25-1	£1.60
8-1	£4.74	10-1	£3.88	30-1	£1.38
8-1	£4.43	12-1	£3.07	15-1	£2.49
8-1	£4.72	12-1	£3.26	20-1	£2.02
8-1	£4.91	12-1	£3.40	25-1	£1.70
8-1	£5.04	12-1	£3.49	30-1	£1.46
8-1	£5.15	12-1	£3.56	35-1	£1.29
8-1	£5.23	12-1	£3.62	40-1	£1.15
10-1	£3.95	12-1	£3.34	15-1	£2.71
10-1	£4.22	12-1	£3.57	20-1	£2.21
10-1	£4.41	12-1	£3.73	25-1	£1.86
10-1	£4.28	16-1	£2.77	15-1	£2.94
10-1	£4.61	16-1	£2.98	20-1	£2.41
10-1	£4.83	16-1	£3.13	25-1	£2.04
12-1	£4.11	15-1	£3.34	20-1	£2.55
12-1	£4.32	15-1	£3.51	25-1	£2.16
12-1	£4.48	15-1	£3.64	30-1	£1.88
15-1	£3.70	16-1	£3.48	20-1	£2.82
15-1	£3.91	16-1	£3.68	25-1	£2.41
15-1	£4.07	16-1	£3.83	30-1	£2.10
15-1	£3.96	20-1	£3.02	20-1	£3.02
15-1	£4.21	20-1	£3.20	25-1	£2.59
15-1	£4.39	20-1	£3.34	30-1	£2.27

THREE AGAINST THE FIELD
(Ante Post Outlay £12)

Odds	Stake	Odds	Stake	Odds	Stake
10-1	£5.14	16-1	£3.33	15-1	£3.53
10-1	£5.53	16-1	£3.58	20-1	£2.90
10-1	£5.80	16-1	£3.75	25-1	£2.45
10-1	£5.99	16-1	£3.88	30-1	£2.13
10-1	£6.15	16-1	£3.98	35-1	£1.88
10-1	£5.43	15-1	£3.73	20-1	£2.84
10-1	£5.69	15-1	£3.91	25-1	£2.41
10-1	£5.88	15-1	£4.04	30-1	£2.08
10-1	£6.02	15-1	£4.14	35-1	£1.84
12-1	£4.66	16-1	£3.56	15-1	£3.78
12-1	£5.03	16-1	£3.85	20-1	£3.12
12-1	£5.30	16-1	£4.05	25-1	£2.65
12-1	£5.49	16-1	£4.20	30-1	£2.30
15-1	£4.44	16-1	£4.18	20-1	£3.38
15-1	£4.69	16-1	£4.42	25-1	£2.89
15-1	£4.88	16-1	£4.60	30-1	£2.52
15-1	£4.75	20-1	£3.62	20-1	£3.62
15-1	£5.05	20-1	£3.85	25-1	£3.11
15-1	£5.27	20-1	£4.01	30-1	£2.72

THREE AGAINST THE FIELD
(Ante Post Outlay £15)

Odds	Stake	Odds	Stake	Odds	Stake
10-1	£5.92	12-1	£5.01	15-1	£4.07
10-1	£6.33	12-1	£5.36	20-1	£3.32
10-1	£6.61	12-1	£5.59	25-1	£2.80
10-1	£6.82	12-1	£5.77	30-1	£2.42
10-1	£6.43	16-1	£4.16	15-1	£4.42
10-1	£6.91	16-1	£4.47	20-1	£3.62
10-1	£7.25	16-1	£4.69	25-1	£3.07
10-1	£7.49	16-1	£4.85	30-1	£2.66
12-1	£5.82	16-1	£4.45	15-1	£4.73
12-1	£6.29	16-1	£4.81	20-1	£3.90
12-1	£6.62	16-1	£5.06	25-1	£3.31
12-1	£6.87	16-1	£5.25	30-1	£2.88
15-1	£5.55	16-1	£5.22	20-1	£4.23
15-1	£5.87	16-1	£5.52	25-1	£3.61
15-1	£6.10	16-1	£5.75	30-1	£3.15
15-1	£6.10	22-1	£4.25	20-1	£4.65
15-1	£6.49	22-1	£4.52	25-1	£3.99
15-1	£6.78	22-1	£4.72	30-1	£3.50
15-1	£5.94	20-1	£4.53	20-1	£4.53
15-1	£6.31	20-1	£4.81	25-1	£3.88
15-1	£6.58	20-1	£5.02	30-1	£3.40

THREE AGAINST THE FIELD
(Ante Post Outlay £20)

Odds	Stake	Odds	Stake	Odds	Stake
10-1	£7.89	12-1	£6.68	15-1	£5.43
10-1	£8.44	12-1	£7.14	20-1	£4.42
10-1	£8.81	12-1	£7.46	25-1	£3.73
10-1	£9.09	12-1	£7.69	30-1	£3.22
10-1	£8.22	15-1	£5.65	25-1	£4.31
10-1	£8.61	15-1	£5.92	30-1	£3.64
10-1	£8.90	15-1	£6.12	35-1	£3.16
10-1	£9.12	15-1	£6.27	40-1	£2.79
10-1	£9.30	15-1	£6.39	45-1	£2.49
10-1	£8.57	16-1	£5.54	15-1	£5.89
10-1	£9.21	16-1	£5.96	20-1	£4.83
10-1	£9.66	16-1	£6.25	25-1	£4.09
10-1	£9.99	16-1	£6.46	30-1	£3.55
12-1	£7.76	16-1	£5.93	15-1	£6.31
12-1	£8.39	16-1	£6.42	20-1	£5.19
12-1	£8.83	16-1	£6.75	25-1	£4.42
12-1	£9.16	16-1	£7.00	30-1	£3.84
15-1	£8.41	20-1	£6.41	25-1	£5.18
15-1	£7.65	20-1	£5.83	30-1	£4.71
15-1	£7.98	20-1	£6.08	35-1	£4.12
15-1	£8.24	20-1	£6.28	40-1	£3.66
15-1	£8.45	20-1	£6.44	45-1	£3.30
15-1	£8.14	22-1	£5.66	20-1	£6.20
15-1	£8.65	22-1	£6.02	25-1	£5.33
15-1	£9.04	22-1	£6.29	30-1	£4.67
15-1	£9.35	22-1	£6.50	35-1	£4.15
16-1	£6.96	15-1	£7.40	20-1	£5.64
16-1	£7.36	15-1	£7.82	25-1	£4.81
16-1	£7.66	15-1	£8.14	30-1	£4.20

THREE AGAINST THE FIELD
(Ante Post Outlay £20)

Odds	Stake	Odds	Stake	Odds	Stake
20-1	£7.32	25-1	£5.91	35-1	£4.96
20-1	£7.60	25-1	£6.14	40-1	£4.44
20-1	£7.84	25-1	£6.33	45-1	£4.01

THREE AGAINST THE FIELD
(Ante Post Outlay £50)

Odds	Stake	Odds	Stake	Odds	Stake
10-1	£20.55	15-1	£14.13	25-1	£10.77
10-1	£21.53	15-1	£14.80	30-1	£9.11
10-1	£22.25	15-1	£15.30	35-1	£7.90
10-1	£22.80	15-1	£15.68	40-1	£6.97
10-1	£23.24	15-1	£15.98	45-1	£6.23
15-1	£18.01	20-1	£13.72	25-1	£13.72
15-1	£19.12	20-1	£14.57	30-1	£11.77
15-1	£19.95	20-1	£15.20	35-1	£10.30
15-1	£20.60	20-1	£15.69	40-1	£9.16
15-1	£21.12	20-1	£16.09	45-1	£8.24
20-1	£16.19	20-1	£16.19	30-1	£13.07
20-1	£16.98	20-1	£16.98	35-1	£11.50
20-1	£17.59	20-1	£17.59	40-1	£10.26
20-1	£18.09	20-1	£18.09	45-1	£9.27
20-1	£18.50	20-1	£18.50	50-1	£8.45
20-1	£18.29	25-1	£14.77	35-1	£12.39
20-1	£19.01	25-1	£15.35	40-1	£11.09
20-1	£19.59	25-1	£15.82	45-1	£10.03
20-1	£20.07	25-1	£16.21	50-1	£9.16
25-1	£16.01	25-1	£16.01	35-1	£13.43
25-1	£16.70	25-1	£16.70	40-1	£12.06
25-1	£17.25	25-1	£17.25	45-1	£10.94
25-1	£17.72	25-1	£17.72	50-1	£10.01

And again I encourage you to work through the more sophisticated version of Three Against — Tax Paid On. In fact I am doing more than encouraging you because I am not including a full Staking Table for this bet, so you will need to use it if you are to make some tables up yourself.

SET AMOUNT OF OUTLAY
(Three Against the Field)
TAX PAID ON

THE EXAMPLE BET

> Runner A 4-1
>
> Runner B 5-1
>
> Runner C 6-1
>
> Set limit £10

ELEMENTS OF FORMULAE

Set Limit $\quad\quad\quad\quad\quad\quad$ = $\quad$ L

Total Stake: £'s Bet $\quad\quad$ = $\quad$ **Ts**: $([T] \times 100) \div 110 = £9.09$

Tax (10% of £'s Bet): $\quad$ = $\quad$ **Tx**: $(T) \div (Ts) = £0.91$

Runner A Odds $\quad\quad\quad$ = $\quad$ **A**

Runner B Odds $\quad\quad\quad$ = $\quad$ **B**

Runner C Odds $\quad\quad\quad$ = $\quad$ **C**

Total Stake **TS** $\quad\quad\quad$ = $\quad$ $([T] \times [100]) \div 110$
$\quad\quad\quad\quad\quad\quad\quad\quad\quad\quad$ $([£10] \times [100]) \div 110$
$\quad\quad\quad\quad\quad\quad\quad\quad\quad\quad$ £9.90

Tax (@ 10% or · 10) Tx $\;$ = $\quad$ $(T - Ts)$
$\quad\quad\quad\quad\quad\quad\quad\quad\quad\quad$ $(10 - 9.09)$
$\quad\quad\quad\quad\quad\quad\quad\quad\quad\quad$ ·91p

Stake Proportion Runner **A** $\quad$ = $\quad$ S1 : $([B+1] \times [C+1])$
$\quad\quad\quad\quad\quad\quad\quad\quad\quad\quad\quad\quad\quad\quad$ $([5+1] \times [6+1])$
$\quad\quad\quad\quad\quad\quad\quad\quad\quad\quad\quad\quad\quad\quad$ (6×7)
$\quad\quad\quad\quad\quad\quad\quad\quad\quad\quad\quad\quad\quad\quad$ $42 = S1$

Stake Proportion Runner **B** $=$ S2 : ([**A**+1] $\times$ [**C**+1])
([4+1] $\times$ [6+1])
(5 $\times$ 7)
35 = S2

Stake Proportion Runner **C** $=$ S3 : ([**A**+1] $\times$ [**B**+1])
([4+1] $\times$ [5+1])
(5 $\times$ 6)
30 = S3

Runners in Combination $=$ S4: ([S1]+[S2]+[S3])
(42 + 35 + 30)
107 = S4

FORMULAE

Runner A: **A** Stake $=$ ([S1]$\times$[**TS**]) $\div$ (S4)
([42]$\times$[9.09]) $\div$ (107)
(371.78) $\div$ (107)
£3.57 = **A**

Runner B: **B** Stake $=$ ([S2]$\times$[**TS**]) $\div$ (S4)
([33]$\times$[9.09]) $\div$ (107)
(318.15) $\div$ (107)
£2.97 = **B**

Runner C: **C** Stake $=$ ([S3]$\times$[**TS**]) $\div$ (S4)
([30]$\times$[9.09]) $\div$ (107)
(272.70) $\div$ (107)
£2.55 = **C**

Total Stake £9.09

Runners	Odds	Stake	Return	Profit
A	4-1	£3.57	£17.85	£7.85
B	5-1	£2.97	£17.82	£7.82
C	6-1	£2.55	£17.85	£7.85
	Total stake	£9.09		
	Tax @ 10%	£0.91		
	Total outlay	£10.00		

The set amount method can of course be applied to more than three horses against the field, but does involve the backer in quite complex calculations.

Therefore, here is a simplified method of betting on quite a few horses taking outlay as your starting point. First, add one to the odds on offer for each of your selections, as in the basic formula. Then divide the result for each into an amount you decide is a reasonable return from your series of bets. This gives you the stake for each horse. To determine your profit in advance, add together the stakes and deduct the total from the specified return.

Here is an example for an ante post race:

Runner A	10-1
Runner B	10-1
Runner C	16-1
Runner D	20-1
Runner E	25-1
Proposed Return £25	

Your series of bets is as follows:

Runner A £25 divided by (10 + 1) = £2.27
Runner B £25 divided by (10 + 1) = £2.27
Runner C £25 divided by (16 + 1) = £1.47
Runner D £25 divided by (20 + 1) = £1.19
Runner E £25 divided by (25 + 1) = £0.96

Total outlay £8.16
Return £25.00
Net profit (before tax) £16.84

So you make a profit of £16.84 whichever of your five selections wins for a total stake on the race of £8.16 before tax.

This variation of the formula does not fulfil specific objectives as precisely as earlier versions in the preceding pages. Also it takes a little practice to relate the specified return to how much you intend to stake. With practice however, you will find it a convenient way of extending the formula to quite a lot of horses in the same race without the necessity for lengthy calculations. The point of course is that once again you proportion your stakes in the way most likely to prove advantageous to yourself at the probable expense of the bookmaker!

Finally, I am including the Tax Paid On working Formulae for Four Against and Six Against the Field. Again, no staking tables because the page does run out of space when all of these columns have to be accommodated! You may well feel that the Basic formula on page 123 is enough to be getting on with, but here you have the *real* thing for future reference should you need them.

SET AMOUNT OF OUTLAY
(Four Against the Field)
TAX PAID ON

THE EXAMPLE BET

> Runner **A** 4-1
> Runner **B** 5-1
> Runner **C** 6-1
> Runner **D** 8-1
>
> Set limit £10

ELEMENTS OF FORMULAE

Set Limit	=	**L**
Total Stake: £'s Bet	=	**Ts**: $([L] \times 100) \div 110 = £9.09$
Tax (10% of £'s Bet):	=	**Tx**: $(L) \div (Ts) = £0.91$
Runner A Odds	=	**A**
Runner B Odds	=	**B**
Runner C Odds	=	**C**
Runner D Odds	=	**D**

Stake Proportion Runner **A**   =   S1:([**B**+1]×[**C**+1])×[**D**+1]
([5+1]×[6+1])×[8+1]
(42 × 9)
378 = S1

Stake Proportion Runner **B**   =   S2:([**A**+1]×[**C**+1])×[**D**+1]
([4+1]×[6+1])×[8+1]
(35 × 9)
315 = S2

Stake Proportion Runner **C**   =   S3:([**A**+1]×[**B**+1])×[**D**+1]
([4+1]×[5+1])×[8+1]
(30 × 9)
270 = S3

Stake Proportion Runner **D**   =   S3:([**A**+1]×[**B**+1])×[**C**+1]
([4+1]×[5+1])×[6+1]
(30 × 7)
210 = S4

Runners in Combination   =   S5:([S1]+[S2]+[S3]+[S4])
(378+315+270+210)
1173 = S5

FORMULAE

Runner A: Stake A   =   ([S1]×[**Ts**])÷[S5]
([378]×[9.09])÷(1173)
(3436 ÷ 1173)
£2.93 = A

Runner B: Stake B   =   ([S2]×[**Ts**])÷[S5]
([315]×[9.09])÷(1173)
£2.44 = B

Runner C: Stake C   =   ([S3]×[**Ts**]÷[S5])
([270]×[9.09]÷(1173)
£2.09 = C

Runner **D**: Stake **D**   =   ([S4]×[**Ts**])÷[S5]
                                     ([210]×[9.09])÷(1173)
                                     £1.63 = Ds

Total Stake = £9.09

Runners	Odds	Stake	Return	Profit
A	4-1	£2.93	£14.65	£4.65
B	5-1	£2.44	£14.64	£4.64
C	6-1	£2.09	£14.63	£4.63
D	8-1	£1.63	£14.67	£4.67
	Total stake	£9.09		
	Tax @ 10%	£0.91		
	Total outlay	£10.00		

SET AMOUNT OF OUTLAY
(Six Against the Field)
TAX PAID ON

THE EXAMPLE BET

Runner A 10-1
Runner B 15-1
Runner C 20-1
Runner D 20-1
Runner E 25-1
Runner F 25-1

Set limit £20

ELEMENTS OF FORMULAE

Set Limit $\quad\quad$ = $\quad$ **L**
Total Stake: £'s Bet = $\quad$ **Ts**: ([**L**]×100) ÷ 110 = £18.18
Tax (10% of £'s Bet):= $\quad$ **Tx**: (**L**) ÷ (**Ts**) = £1.82
Runner A Odds $\quad$ = $\quad$ **A**
Runner B Odds $\quad$ = $\quad$ **B**
Runner C Odds $\quad$ = $\quad$ **C**
Runner D Odds $\quad$ = $\quad$ **D**
Runner E Odds $\quad$ = $\quad$ **E**
Runner F Odds $\quad$ = $\quad$ **F**

Stake Proportion Runner **A**
$\quad$ = $\quad$ S1: ([**B**+1]×[**C**+1]×[**D**+1]×[**E**+1]×[**F**+1])
$\quad\quad\quad\quad$ ([15+1]×[20+1]×[20+1]×[25+1]×[25+1])
$\quad\quad\quad\quad$ (16 × 21 × 21 × 26 × 26)
$\quad\quad\quad\quad$ **4,769,856 = S1**

Stake Proportion Runner **B**
$\quad$ = $\quad$ S2: ([**B**+1]×[**C**+1]×[**D**+1]×[**E**+1]×[**F**+1])
$\quad\quad\quad\quad$ ([10+1]×[20+1]×[20+1]×[25+1]×[25+1])
$\quad\quad\quad\quad$ (11 × 21 × 21 × 26 × 26)
$\quad\quad\quad\quad$ **3,279,276 = S2**

Stake Proportion Runner C

$$= \text{S3:} \quad ([A+1]\times[B+1]\times[D+1]\times[E+1]\times[F+1])$$
$$([10+1]\times[15+1]\times[20+1]\times[25+1]\times[25+1])$$
$$(11 \times 16 \times 21 \times 26 \times 26)$$
$$\mathbf{2,498,496 = S3}$$

Stake Proportion Runner D

$$= \text{S4:} \quad ([A+1]\times[B+1]\times[C+1]\times[E+1]\times[F+1])$$
$$([10+1]\times[15+1]\times[20+1]\times[25+1]\times[25+1])$$
$$(11 \times 16 \times 21 \times 26 \times 26)$$
$$\mathbf{2,489,496 = S4}$$

Stake Proportion Runner E

$$= \text{S5:} \quad ([D+1]\times[A+1]\times[B+1]\times[C+1]\times[F+1])$$
$$([20+1]\times[10+1]\times[15+1]\times[20+1]\times[25+1])$$
$$(21 \times 11 \times 16 \times 21 \times 26)$$
$$\mathbf{2,018,016 = S5}$$

Stake Proportion Runner F

$$= \text{S6:} \quad ([A+1]\times[B+1]\times[C+1]\times[D+1]\times[E+1])$$
$$([10+1]\times[15+1]\times[20+1]\times[20+1]\times[25+1])$$
$$(11 \times 16 \times 21 \times 21 \times 26)$$
$$\mathbf{2,018,016 = S6}$$

Staking Factor = **S** = (S1+S2+S3+S4+S5+S6)
S = **17,082,156**

FORMULAE
Stake for Runner A =
$$(4,769,856 \times £18.18) \div 17,082,156$$
$$86,715,982 \div 17,082,156$$

Stake for Runner A = £5.0̇8

If you now replace S1 with S2 in the Formula you will produce the stake for B. Then S3 in the Formula will produce you C, etc. All the way down to F. To save you the trouble, they will work out like this!

A @ £5.08	C @ £2.66	E @ £2.14
B @ £3.50	D @ £2.66	F @ £2.14

Total Stake = £18.18

Runners	Odds	Stake	Return	Profit
A	10-1	£5.08	£55.88	£35.88
B	15-1	£3.50	£56.00	£36.00
C	20-1	£2.66	£55.86	£35.86
D	20-1	£2.66	£55.86	£35.86
E	25-1	£2.14	£55.90	£35.90
F	25-1	£2.14	£55.90	£35.90
	Total stake	£18.08		
	Tax @ 10%	£1.82		
	Total outlay	£20.00		

The
Computer
Programmes

How to Handle the Computer Programmes

The following pages contain *10* computer programs. The programs are compatible with most types of BASIC including GWBASIC and will run on IBM compatible computers.

To enter the progams boot up your PC and type GWBASIC. This will make the machine ready to receive your typing.

Type in the program of your choice by copying each line, including the number at the beginning. At the end of each line press RETURN. Be careful to type each listing *exactly* as printed.

Save the program to disc periodically by typing SAVE"PROG", where PROG is the name of the listing. For example, to save Listing 1, type SAVE"3FIELD". When you have finished type SAVE"PROG" one more time.

To run your program type CHAIN"PROG", where PROG is the name of the file. For example, to run listing 1 after you have entered it type CHAIN"3FIELD".

Note: To enter pound signs (£) hold down the Alt key, type 156 on the numeric keypad of the keyboard, and then let go of the Alt key. A pound sign will appear.

The Programmes

1   Three Against — To Win the Same Amount   135

2   Three Against — Descending Value of Winnings 138

3   Three Against — One Winner & Two Savers   141

4   Four Against — To Win the Same Amount   144

5   Four Against — One Winner & Three Savers   148

6   Four Against — Two Winners & Two Savers   151

7   Five Against — To Win the Same Amount   157

8   Five Against — One to Win & Four Savers   161

9   Five Against — Two Winners & Three Savers   167

10 Six Against — To Win the Same Amount   171

In General

There are several places where you will see a VDU command. This command is not used in many types of basic and should be removed. In some cases it is preceeded by a REM statement which is fine as this means that the line is ignored.

Spaces

Different versions of basic have different requirements for spaces between commands. `PRINT TAB(8)` and `PRINTTAB(8)` may look the same but to QBasic for instance the first version makes no sense. Your version of basic may automatically put the spaces where it needs them but if it doesn't you'll have to insert them in the correct place yourself. Look in your manual to find out how your version of Basic requires spaces.

Commas and semicolons

Placing of Commas and semicolons is as important as the placing of spaces. Again whether they are needed or not depends on the version of basic you are using. QBasic for instance has to have a semi colon after the Input String and before the input variable. For instance :-

```
100 INPUT"Odds for Runner A";A
```
will work, but

```
100 INPUT"Odds for Runner A"A
```
will not

Again, look in your manual to find out how you version of Basic requires commas and semi colons.

Printing the results of the programmes

You might like to output the results of the programmes to a printer. Some of the programmes are designed for a screen width of 80 characters and final results may look a little messy on a screen that is 40 characters wide. Printers are often 80 or more characters wide.

A common way of sending output to the printer in a basic programme is to replace the PRINT statement with LPRINT, but please check this for your version of Basic.

APPENDIX

Computer Program 1

Save and Run as "3FIELD"

PROGRAMME 1 - 3FIELD

```
10 CLS : PRINT ""
12 PRINT TAB(8); "THREE AGAINST THE FIELD"
14 PRINT TAB(8); "========================"
15 PRINT
20 INPUT "ODDS OF RUNNER A ", ODDSA
30 INPUT "ODDS OF RUNNER B ", ODDSB
40 INPUT "ODDS OF RUNNER C ", ODDSC
45 PRINT
50 INPUT "PROFIT FROM RUNNER A £", PROFITA
60 INPUT "PROFIT FROM RUNNER B £", PROFITB
70 INPUT "PROFIT FROM RUNNER C £", PROFITC
72 PRINT ""
74 INPUT "PRESS RETURN TO CONTINUE", V
76 CLS : PRINT ""
80 S = ((ODDSB * ODDSC) - 1) * PROFITA
90 S1 = ((ODDSC + 1)) * PROFITB
100 S2 = ((ODDSB + 1) * PROFITC)
110 S3 = S + S1 + S2
120 S4 = ((ODDSA * ODDSB * ODDSC) - (ODDSA + ODDSB + ODDSC)) - 2
130 S15 = S3 / S4
140 S5 = INT(S15 * 100 + .5) / 100 + .05
150 REM ...S5 IS STAKE FOR RUNNER A
160 S6 = ((ODDSC * ODDSA) - 1) * PROFITB
170 S7 = ((ODDSA + 1) * (PROFITC))
180 S8 = ((ODDSC + 1) * (PROFITA))
190 S9 = S6 + S7 + S8
200 S110 = S9 / S4
210 S10 = INT(S110 * 100 + .5) / 100 + .05
```

```
220 REM ...S10 IS STAKE FOR RUNNER B
230 S11 = ((ODDSA * ODDSB) - 1) * PROFITC
240 S12 = (ODDSB + 1) * PROFITA
250 S13 = (ODDSA + 1) * PROFITB
260 S14 = S11 + S12 + S13
270 S115 = S14 / S4
280 S15 = INT(S115 * 100 + .05) / 100 + .05
290 REM ..S15 IS STAKE FOR RUNNER C
300 T = S5 + S10 + S15
310 T11 = T / 10
312 T1 = INT(T11 * 100 + .5) / 100
320 REM ..T IS TOTAL STAKES
330 T2 = T + T1
340 R = (ODDSA + 1) * S5
350 R1 = (ODDSB + 1) * S10
360 R2 = (ODDSC + 1) * S15
370 PRINT
380 PRINT
390 P = R - T
400 P1 = R1 - T
410 P2 = R2 - T
420 PRINT
425 PRINT TAB(8); "THREE AGAINST THE FIELD"
430 PRINT TAB(8); "======================="
440 PRINT TAB(2); "ODDS"; TAB(10); "STAKE"; TAB(20); "RETURN";
    TAB(29); "PROFIT"
450 PRINT TAB(2); "===================================="
460 PRINT TAB(2); "(A)"; ODDSA; "/1"; TAB(10); "£"; S5; TAB(20); "£"; R
    TAB(29); "£"; P
470 PRINT TAB(2); "(B)"; ODDSB; "/1"; TAB(10); "£"; S10; TAB(20); "£";
    TAB(29); "£"; P1
480 PRINT TAB(2); "(C)"; ODDSC; "/1"; TAB(10); "£"; S15; TAB(20); "£";
    TAB(29); "£"; P2
490 PRINT TAB(10); "=========="
500 PRINT TAB(2); "TOTAL"
510 PRINT TAB(2); "STAKES"; TAB(10); "£"; T
520 PRINT TAB(2); "TAX"; TAB(10); "£"; T1
530 PRINT TAB(10); "=========="
```

```
540 PRINT TAB(2); "TOTAL"
550 PRINT TAB(2); "OUTLAY"; TAB(10); "£"; T2
560 PRINT TAB(10); "=========="
570 PRINT
580 PRINT TAB(2); "TOTAL OUTLAY (INC. TAX) £"; T2; "."
590 PRINT
600 PRINT TAB(2); "IF RUNNER A WINS, PROFIT £"; P; "."
610 PRINT TAB(2); "IF RUNNER B WINS, PROFIT £"; P1; "."
620 PRINT TAB(2); "IF RUNNER C WINS, PROFIT £"; P2; "."
622 PRINT
```

THREE AGAINST THE FIELD

Runners	Odds	Stake	Return	Profit
A	10-1	£2.33	£25.83	£20.45
B	15-1	£1.61	£25.76	£20.58
C	20-1	£1.24	£26.04	£20.86
	Stakes	£5.18		
	Tax	£0.52		
	Total outlay	£5.70		

Total outlay (including tax) £5.70.
If Runner A wins, profit £20.45.
If Runner B wins, profit £20.58.
If Runner C wins, profit £20.86.

Computer Program 2

Save and Run as "3DESC"

PROGRAMME 2 - 3DESC

```
10 CLS : PRINT ""
12 PRINT TAB(8); "THREE AGAINST THE FIELD"
14 PRINT TAB(8); "========================="
15 PRINT
20 INPUT "ODDS OF RUNNER A ", ODDSA
30 INPUT "ODDS OF RUNNER B ", ODDSB
40 INPUT "ODDS OF RUNNER C ", ODDSC
45 PRINT
50 INPUT "PROFIT FROM RUNNER A £", PROFITA
60 INPUT "PROFIT FROM RUNNER B £", PROFITB
70 INPUT "PROFIT FROM RUNNER C £", PROFITC
72 PRINT ""
74 INPUT "PRESS RETURN TO CONTINUE", V
76 CLS : PRINT ""
80 S = ((ODDSB * ODDSC) - 1) * PROFITA
90 S1 = ((ODDSC + 1)) * PROFITB
100 S2 = ((ODDSB + 1) * PROFITC)
110 S3 = S + S1 + S2
120 S4 = ((ODDSA * ODDSB * ODDSC) - (ODDSA + ODDSB + ODDSC))
130 S15 = S3 / S4
140 S5 = INT(S15 * 100 + .5) / 100 + .05
150 REM ...S5 IS STAKE FOR RUNNER A
160 S6 = ((ODDSC * ODDSA) - 1) * PROFITB
170 S7 = ((ODDSA + 1) * (PROFITC))
180 S8 = ((ODDSC + 1) * (PROFITA))
190 S9 = S6 + S7 + S8
200 S110 = S9 / S4
210 S10 = INT(S110 * 100 + .5) / 100 + .05
220 REM ...S10 IS STAKE FOR RUNNER B
230 S11 = ((ODDSA * ODDSB) - 1) * PROFITC
240 S12 = (ODDSB + 1) * PROFITA
250 S13 = (ODDSA + 1) * PROFITB
260 S14 = S11 + S12 + S13
```

```
270 S115 = S14 / S4
280 S15 = INT(S115 * 100 + .05) / 100 + .05
290 REM ..S15 IS STAKE FOR RUNNER C
300 T = S5 + S10 + S15
310 T11 = T / 10
312 T1 = INT(T11 * 100 + .5) / 100
320 REM ..T IS TOTAL STAKES
330 T2 = T + T1
340 R = (ODDSA + 1) * S5
350 R1 = (ODDSB + 1) * S10
360 R2 = (ODDSC + 1) * S15
370 PRINT
380 PRINT
390 P = R - T
400 P1 = R1 - T
410 P2 = R2 - T
420 PRINT
425 PRINT TAB(8); "THREE AGAINST THE FIELD"
430 PRINT TAB(8); "========================"
440 PRINT TAB(2); "ODDS"; TAB(10); "STAKE"; TAB(20); "RETURN";
    TAB(29); "PROFIT"
450 PRINT TAB(2); "================================="
460 PRINT TAB(2); "(A)"; ODDSA; "/1"; TAB(10); "£"; S5; TAB(20); "£"; R;
    TAB(29); "£"; P
470 PRINT TAB(2); "(B)"; ODDSB; "/1"; TAB(10); "£"; S10; TAB(20); "£"; R1;
    TAB(29); "£"; P1
480 PRINT TAB(2); "(C)"; ODDSC; "/1"; TAB(10); "£"; S15; TAB(20); "£"; R2;
    TAB(29); "£"; P2
490 PRINT TAB(10); "=========="
500 PRINT TAB(2); "TOTAL"
510 PRINT TAB(2); "STAKES"; TAB(10); "£"; T
520 PRINT TAB(2); "TAX"; TAB(10); "£"; T1
530 PRINT TAB(10); "=========="
540 PRINT TAB(2); "TOTAL"
550 PRINT TAB(2); "OUTLAY"; TAB(10); "£"; T2
560 PRINT TAB(10); "=========="
570 PRINT
580 PRINT TAB(2); "TOTAL OUTLAY (INC. TAX) £"; T2; "."
```

```
590 PRINT
600 PRINT TAB(2); "IF RUNNER A WINS, PROFIT £"; P; "."
610 PRINT TAB(2); "IF RUNNER B WINS, PROFIT £"; P1; "."
620 PRINT TAB(2); "IF RUNNER C WINS, PROFIT £"; P2; "."
622 PRINT
```

THREE AGAINST THE FIELD

Runners	Odds	Stake	Return	Profit
A	10-1	£3.28	£36.08	£30.36
B	15-1	£1.65	£26.40	£20.68
C	20-1	£0.79	£16.59	£10.87
	Stakes	£5.72		
	Tax	£0.57		
	Total outlay	£6.29		

Total outlay (including tax) £6.29.
If Runner A wins, profit £30.36.
If Runner B wins, profit £20.68.
If Runner C wins, profit £10.87.

Computer Program 3

Save and Run as "3(1+2)"

PROGRAMME 3 - 3(1+2)
```
10 CLS : PRINT "'
12 PRINT TAB(8); "THREE AGAINST THE FIELD"
14 PRINT TAB(8); "========================="
15 PRINT
20 INPUT "ODDS OF RUNNER A ", ODDSA
30 INPUT "ODDS OF RUNNER B ", ODDSB
40 INPUT "ODDS OF RUNNER C ", ODDSC
45 PRINT
50 INPUT "PROFIT FROM RUNNER A £", PROFITA
60 INPUT "PROFIT FROM RUNNER B £", PROFITB
70 INPUT "PROFIT FROM RUNNER C £", PROFITC
72 PRINT "'
74 INPUT "PRESS RETURN TO CONTINUE", V
76 CLS : PRINT "'
80 S = ((ODDSB * ODDSC) - 1) * PROFITA
90 S1 = ((ODDSC + 1)) * PROFITB
100 S2 = ((ODDSB + 1) * PROFITC)
110 S3 = S + S1 + S2
120 S4 = ((ODDSA * ODDSB * ODDSC) - (ODDSA + ODDSB + ODDSC)) - 2
130 S15 = S3 / S4
140 S5 = INT(S15 * 100 + .5) / 100 + .05
150 REM ...S5 IS STAKE FOR RUNNER A
160 S6 = ((ODDSC * ODDSA) - 1) * PROFITB
170 S7 = ((ODDSA + 1) * (PROFITC))
180 S8 = ((ODDSC + 1) * (PROFITA))
190 S9 = S6 + S7 + S8
200 S110 = S9 / S4
210 S10 = INT(S110 * 100 + .5) / 100 + .05
220 REM ...S10 IS STAKE FOR RUNNER B
230 S11 = ((ODDSA * ODDSB) - 1) * PROFITC
240 S12 = (ODDSB + 1) * PROFITA
250 S13 = (ODDSA + 1) * PROFITB
260 S14 = S11 + S12 + S13
```

```
270 S115 = S14 / S4
280 S15 = INT(S115 * 100 + .05) / 100 + .05
290 REM ..S15 IS STAKE FOR RUNNER C
300 T = S5 + S10 + S15
310 T11 = T / 10
312 T1 = INT(T11 * 100 + .5) / 100
320 REM ..T IS TOTAL STAKES
330 T2 = T + T1
340 R = (ODDSA + 1) * S5
350 R1 = (ODDSB + 1) * S10
360 R2 = (ODDSC + 1) * S15
370 PRINT
380 PRINT
390 P = R - T
400 P1 = R1 - T
410 P2 = R2 - T
420 PRINT
425 PRINT TAB(8); "THREE AGAINST THE FIELD"
430 PRINT TAB(8); "======================="
440 PRINT TAB(2); "ODDS"; TAB(10); "STAKE"; TAB(20); "RETURN";
      TAB(29); "PROFIT"
450 PRINT TAB(2); "===================================="
460 PRINT TAB(2); "(A)"; ODDSA; "/1"; TAB(10); "£"; S5; TAB(20); "£"; R;
      TAB(29); "£"; P
470 PRINT TAB(2); "(B)"; ODDSB; "/1"; TAB(10); "£"; S10; TAB(20); "£"; F
      TAB(29); "£"; P1
480 PRINT TAB(2); "(C)"; ODDSC; "/1"; TAB(10); "£"; S15; TAB(20); "£"; F
      TAB(29); "£"; P2
490 PRINT TAB(10); "========="
500 PRINT TAB(2); "TOTAL"
510 PRINT TAB(2); "STAKES"; TAB(10); "£"; T
520 PRINT TAB(2); "TAX"; TAB(10); "£"; T1
530 PRINT TAB(10); "========="
540 PRINT TAB(2); "TOTAL"
550 PRINT TAB(2); "OUTLAY"; TAB(10); "£"; T2
560 PRINT TAB(10); "========="
570 PRINT
580 PRINT TAB(2); "TOTAL OUTLAY (INC. TAX) £"; T2; "."
```

```
590 PRINT
600 PRINT TAB(2); "IF RUNNER A WINS, PROFIT £"; P; "."
610 PRINT TAB(2); "IF RUNNER B WINS, PROFIT £"; P1; "."
620 PRINT TAB(2); "IF RUNNER C WINS, PROFIT £"; P2; "."
622 PRINT
```

THREE AGAINST THE FIELD

Runners	Odds	Stake	Return	Profit
A	10-1	£4.35	£47.85	£40.39
B	15-1	£1.76	£28.16	£20.70
C	20-1	£1.35	£28.35	£20.89
	Stakes	£7.46		
	Tax	£0.75		
	Total outlay	£8.21		

Total outlay (including tax) £8.21.
If Runner A wins, profit £40.39.
If Runner B wins, profit £20.70.
If Runner C wins, profit £20.89.

Computer Program 4

Save and Run as "4FIELD"

PROGRAMME 4 - 4FIELD

```
10 CLS
20 PRINT ""
25 PRINT TAB(6); "FOUR AGAINST THE FIELD"
130 INPUT "ODDS OF RUNNER A "; ODDSA
140 INPUT "ODDS OF RUNNER B "; ODDSB
150 INPUT "ODDS OF RUNNER C "; ODDSC
160 INPUT "ODDS OF RUNNER D "; ODDSD
170 PRINT
180 INPUT "PROFIT FROM TEAM A/B £"; P1
190 INPUT "PROFIT FROM TEAM C/D £"; P2
210 T = .1: P1 = P1: P2 = P2
220 H = ((ODDSA * ODDSB) - 1)
230 H1 = ((ODDSA + ODDSB) + 2)
240 H2 = H / H1
250 O1 = H2
260 H3 = ((ODDSC * ODDSD) - 1)
270 H4 = ((ODDSC + ODDSD) + 2)
280 H5 = H3 / H4
290 O2 = H5
300 S = P1 * (O2 - T) + ((P2) * (1.1))
310 S1 = ((O1 - T) * (O2 - T)) - (1.21)
320 S2 = S / S1
330 S3 = ((P2) * (O1 - T)) + ((P1) * (1.1))
340 S4 = ((O2 - T) * (O1 - T)) - (1.21)
350 S5 = S3 / S4
360 S6 = S2 + S5
370 H6 = S6 / 10
380 R1 = ((O1) + (1)) * (S2)
390 R2 = ((O2) + 1) * (S5)
400 H17 = ((ODDSB + 1) * (S2)) / ((ODDSA + ODDSB) + (2))
410 H7 = INT(H17 * 100 + .5) / 100 + .01
420 H11 = INT(H7 * 100 + .5) / 100
```

```
430 H18 = ((ODDSA + 1) * (S2)) / ((ODDSA + ODDSB) + (2))
440 H8 = INT(H18 * 100 + .5) / 100 + .01
450 H12 = INT(H8 * 100 + .5) / 100
460 H19 = ((ODDSD + 1) * (S5)) / ((ODDSC + ODDSD) + (2))
470 H9 = INT(H19 * 100 + .5) / 100 + .01
480 H13 = INT(H9 * 100 + .5) / 100
490 H21 = ((ODDSC + 1) * (S5)) / ((ODDSC + ODDSD) + (2))
500 H10 = INT(H21 * 100 + .5) / 100 + .01
510 H14 = INT(H10 * 100 + .5) / 100
520 H15 = (H11) + (H12) + (H13) + (H14)
530 H16 = (H15) / 10
540 J15 = INT(H16 * 100 + .5) / 100
550 J16 = INT(H16 * 100 + .5) / 100
560 H17 = H15 + H16
570 E1 = INT(H17 * 100 + .5) / 100
580 J1 = H7 + H8 + H9 + H10
590 E = INT(J1 * 100 + .5) / 100
600 J2 = ((J1) / (10))
610 J33 = (ODDSA + 1) * (H7): J3 = INT(J33 * 100 + .5) / 100
620 J10 = INT(J3 * 100 + .5) / 100
630 J4 = (ODDSB + 1) * H8
640 J11 = INT(J4 * 100 + .5) / 100
650 J55 = (ODDSC + 1) * (H9): J5 = INT(J55 * 100 + .5) / 100
660 J12 = INT(J5 * 100 + .5) / 100
670 J66 = (ODDSD + 1) * (H10): J6 = INT(J66 * 100 + .5) / 100
680 J13 = INT(J6 * 100 + .5) / 100
690 J77 = J1 / 10: J7 = INT(J77 * 100 + .5) / 100
700 K99 = J1 + J7: K = INT(K99 * 100 + .5) / 100
710 K1 = J3 - K
720 K222 = J4 - K: K2 = INT(K222 * 100 + .5) / 100
730 K333 = J5 - K: K3 = INT(K333 * 100 + .5) / 100
740 K444 = J6 - K: K4 = INT(K444 * 100 + .5) / 100
810 PRINT
820 PRINT TAB(6); "FOUR AGAINST THE FIELD"
830 PRINT TAB(7); "(PROFIT TARGET £"; P1; ")"
840 PRINT TAB(2); "================================="
850 PRINT TAB(2); "ODDS"; TAB(9); "STAKE"; TAB(17); "RETURN"; TAB(25);
    "PROFIT"
860 PRINT TAB(2); "================================="
```

```
870 PRINT TAB(2); ODDSA; "/1"; TAB(9); "£"; H7; TAB(17); "£"; J3; TAB(2!
    "£"; K1
880 PRINT TAB(2); ODDSB; "/1"; TAB(9); "£"; H8; TAB(17); "£"; J4; TAB(2!
    "£"; K2
890 PRINT TAB(2); ODDSC; "/1"; TAB(9); "£"; H9; TAB(17); "£"; J5; TAB(2!
    "£"; K3
900 PRINT TAB(2); ODDSD; "/1"; TAB(9); "£"; H10; TAB(17); "£"; J6; TAB(
    "£"; K4
910 PRINT TAB(9); "=========="
920 PRINT TAB(2); "TOTAL"
930 PRINT TAB(2); "STAKES"; TAB(9); "£"; J1
940 PRINT TAB(2); "TAX"; TAB(9); "£"; J7
950 PRINT TAB(9); "=========="
960 PRINT TAB(2); "TOTAL"
970 PRINT TAB(2); "OUTLAY"; TAB(9); "£"; K
980 PRINT TAB(9); "=========="
990 PRINT
993 PRINT TAB(2); "TOTAL OUTLAY £"; K
995 PRINT
1000 PRINT TAB(2); "IF ANY ONE OF THE FOUR"
1010 PRINT TAB(2); "SELECTION IS THE"
1020 PRINT TAB(2); "WINNER: NET PROFIT £"; P1
```

FOUR AGAINST THE FIELD
(Profit Target £50)

Runners	Odds	Stake	Return	Profit
A	10-1	£6.18	£67.98	£50.06
B	15-1	£4.25	£68.00	£50.08
C	20-1	£3.24	£68.04	£50.12
D	25-1	£2.62	£68.12	£50.20
	Stakes	£16.29		
	Tax	£1.63		
	Total outlay	£17.92		

Total outlay £17.92.
If any one of the four selections is the winner, net profit £50.

Computer Program 5

Save and Run as "4(1+3)"

PROGRAMME 5 - 4(1+3)
```
10 PRINT TAB(2); "FOUR AGAINST THE FIELD"
15 PRINT TAB(2); "======================="
30 INPUT "ODDS OF RUNNER A "; ODDSA
40 INPUT "ODDS OF RUNNER B "; ODDSB
50 INPUT "ODDS OF RUNNER C "; ODDSC
60 INPUT "ODDS OF RUNNER D "; ODDSD
70 PRINT '
80 INPUT "PROFIT FROM RUNNER A £"; P1
90 INPUT "PROFIT FROM TEAM (B/C/D): £"; P2
100 PRINT "'
110 INPUT "PRESS RETURN TO CONTINUE "; V
120 CLS
130 PRINT "'
140 T = .1
150 R = (ODDSD + 1) * (ODDSC + 1)
160 R1 = (ODDSD + 1) * (ODDSB + 1)
170 R2 = (ODDSB + 1) * (ODDSC + 1)
180 R3 = R + R1 + R2
190 R4 = (ODDSB + 1) * R
200 R5 = R4 - R3
210 R6 = R5 / R3
220 R7 = INT(R6 * 100 + .5) / 100
230 O1 = ODDSA: O2 = R7
240 S = ((P1) * (O2 - T)) + ((P2) * (1.1))
250 S1 = ((O1 - T) * (O2 - T)) - 1.21
260 S12 = S / S1
270 S2 = INT(S12 * 100 + .5) / 100 + .01
280 S3 = ((P2) * (O1 - T)) + ((P1) * (1.1))
290 S4 = ((O2 - T) * (O1 - T)) - 1.21
300 S5 = S3 / S4
310 S6 = S2 + S5
320 S7 = S6 / 10
```

```
330 S8 = S6 + S7
340 S9 = (ODDSA + 1) * S2
350 S10 = (O2 + 1) * S5
360 S31 = ((R) * (S5)) / R3
370 S11 = INT(S31 * 100 + .5) / 100 + .01
380 S32 = ((R1) * (S5)) / R3
390 S12 = INT(S32 * 100 + .5) / 100 + .01
400 S33 = ((R2) * (S5)) / R3
410 S13 = INT(S33 * 100 + .5) / 100 + .01
420 S15 = (ODDSB + 1) * S11
430 S16 = (ODDSC + 1) * S12
440 S17 = (ODDSD + 1) * S13
450 S18 = S2 + S11 + S12 + S13
460 S199 = S18 / 10
462 S19 = INT(S199 * 100 + .5) / 100
470 S20 = S18 + S19
480 F = S9 - S20
490 F1 = S15 - S20
500 F2 = S16 - S20
510 F3 = S17 - S20
515 REM
520 PRINT TAB(2); "FOUR AGAINST THE FIELD"
530 PRINT TAB(2); "========================="
540 PRINT TAB(2); "ODDS"; TAB(10), "STAKE"; TAB(17); "RETURN";
      TAB(25); "PROFIT"
550 PRINT TAB(2); "================================="
560 PRINT TAB(2); "(A)"; ODDSA; "/1"; TAB(10); "£"; S2; TAB(17); "£"; S9;
      TAB(25); "£"; F
570 PRINT TAB(2); "(A)"; ODDSB; "/1"; TAB(10); "£"; S11; TAB(17); "£"; S15;
      TAB(25); "£"; F1
580 PRINT TAB(2); "(A)"; ODDSC; "/1"; TAB(10); "£"; S12; TAB(17); "£"; S16;
      TAB(25); "£"; F2
590 PRINT TAB(2); "(A)"; ODDSD; "/1"; TAB(10); "£"; S13; TAB(17); "£"; S17;
      TAB(25); "£"; F3
600 PRINT TAB(2); "==============================="
610 PRINT TAB(2); "TOTAL"
620 PRINT TAB(2); "STAKES"; TAB(10); "£"; S18
630 PRINT TAB(2); "TAX"; TAB(10); "£"; S19
```

```
640 PRINT TAB(2); "================================="
650 PRINT TAB(2); "TOTAL"
660 PRINT TAB(2); "OUTLAY"; TAB(10); "£"; S20
670 PRINT TAB(2); "================================="
672 PRINT
674 PRINT TAB(2); "TOTAL OUTLAY £"; S20
675 PRINT TAB(2); "WINNER RUNNER A PROFIT £"; F
676 PRINT TAB(2); "WINNER RUNNER B PROFIT £"; F1
677 PRINT TAB(2); "WINNER RUNNER C PROFIT £"; F2
678 PRINT TAB(2); "WINNER RUNNER D PROFIT £"; F3
```

FOUR AGAINST THE FIELD

Runners	Odds	Stake	Return	Profit
A	10-1	£5.37	£59.07	£50.02
B	15-1	£1.20	£19.20	£10.15
C	20-1	£0.92	£19.32	£10.27
D	25-1	£0.74	£19.24	£10.19
	Stakes	£8.23		
	Tax	£0.82		
	Total outlay	£9.05		

Total outlay £9.05.
If Runner A wins, profit £50.02.
If Runner B wins, profit £10.15.
If Runner C wins, profit £10.27.
If Runner D wins, profit £10.19.

Computer Program 6

Save and Run as "4(2+2)"

PROGRAMME 6 - 4(2+2)
```
50 PRINT TAB(2); "FOUR AGAINST THE FIELD"
120 INPUT "ODDS OF RUNNER A "; ODDSA
130 INPUT "ODDS OF RUNNER B "; ODDSB
140 INPUT "ODDS OF RUNNER C "; ODDSC
150 INPUT "ODDS OF RUNNER D "; ODDSD
160 PRINT
170 INPUT "PROFIT FROM TEAM A/B £"; P1
180 INPUT "PROFIT FROM TEAM C/D £"; P2
190 INPUT "NUMBER OF LINES"; Z
200 T = .1
210 H = ((ODDSA * ODDSB) - 1)
220 H1 = ((ODDSA + ODDSB) + 2)
230 H2 = H / H1
240 O1 = H2
250 H3 = ((ODDSC * ODDSD) - 1)
260 H4 = ((ODDSC + ODDSD) + 2)
270 H5 = H3 / H4
280 O2 = H5
290 S = ((P1) * (O2 - T)) + ((P2) * (1.1))
300 S1 = ((O1 - T) * (O2 - T)) - 1.21
310 S2 = S / S1
320 S3 = ((P2) * (O1 - T)) + ((P1) * (1.1))
330 S4 = ((O2 - T) * (O1 - T)) - 1.21
340 S5 = S3 / S4
350 S6 = S2 + S5
360 H6 = S6 / 10
370 R1 = ((O1) + (1)) * S2
380 R2 = ((O2) + 1) * S5
390 H17 = ((ODDSB + 1) * (S2)) / ((ODDSA + ODDSB) + (2))
400 H7 = INT(H17 * 100 + .5) / 100 + .01
410 H11 = INT(H7 * 100 + .5) / 100
420 H18 = ((ODDSA + 1) * (S2)) / ((ODDSA + ODDSB) + (2))
```

```
430 H8 = INT(H18 * 100 + .5) / 100 + .01
440 H12 = INT(H8 * 100 + .5) / 100
450 H19 = ((ODDSD + 1) * (S5)) / ((ODDSC + ODDSD) + (2))
460 H9 = INT(H19 * 100 + .5) / 100 + .01
470 H13 = INT(H9 * 100 + .5) / 100
480 H21 = ((ODDSC + 1) * (S5)) / ((ODDSC + ODDSD) + (2))
490 H10 = INT(H21 * 100 + .5) / 100 + .01
500 H14 = INT(H10 * 100 + .5) / 100
510 H15 = H11 + H12 + H13 + H14
520 H16 = H15 / 10
530 J15 = INT(H16 * 100 + .5) / 100
540 J16 = INT(H16 * 100 + .5) / 100
550 H17 = H15 + H16
560 E1 = INT(H17 * 100 + .5) / 100
570 J1 = H7 + H8 + H9 + H10
580 E = INT(J1 * 100 + .5) / 100
590 J2 = J1 / 10
600 J33 = (ODDSA + 1) * H7: J3 = INT(J33 * 100 + .5) / 100
610 J10 = INT(J3 * 100 + .5) / 100
620 J44 = (ODDSB + 1) * H8: J4 = INT(J44 * 100 + .5) / 100
630 J11 = INT(J4 * 100 + .5) / 100
640 J55 = (ODDSC + 1) * H9: J5 = INT(J55 * 100 + .5) / 100
650 J12 = INT(J5 * 100 + .5) / 100
660 J6 = (ODDSD + 1) * H10
670 J13 = INT(J6 * 100 + .5) / 100
680 J77 = J1 / 10: J7 = INT(J77 * 100 + .5) / 100
690 K99 = J1 + J7: K = INT(K99 * 100 + .5) / 100
700 K1 = J3 - K
710 K2 = J4 - K
720 K3 = J5 - K
730 K4 = J6 - K
740 CLS
750 PRINT ""
760 PRINT TAB(2); "RUNNER A..."; ODDSA; "/1"
770 PRINT TAB(2); "RUNNER B..."; ODDSB; "/1"
780 PRINT TAB(2); "RUNNER C..."; ODDSC; "/1"
790 PRINT TAB(2); "RUNNER D..."; ODDSD; "/1"
800 PRINT
810 PRINT TAB(2); "FOUR AGAINST THE FIELD"
```

```
820 PRINT TAB(2); "======================="
830 PRINT TAB(2); "ODDS"; TAB(9); "STAKE"; TAB(17); "RETURN"; TAB(25)
    "PROFIT"
840 PRINT TAB(2); "================================="
850 PRINT TAB(2); ODDSA; "/1"; TAB(9); "£"; H7; TAB(17); "£"; J3; TAB(25);
    "£"; K1
860 PRINT TAB(2); ODDSB; "/1"; TAB(9); "£"; H8; TAB(17); "£"; J4; TAB(25);
    "£"; K2
870 PRINT TAB(2); ODDSC; "/1"; TAB(9); "£"; H9; TAB(17); "£"; J5; TAB(25);
    "£"; K3
880 PRINT TAB(2); ODDSD; "/1"; TAB(9); "£"; H10; TAB(17); "£"; J6; TAB(25)
    "£"; K4
890 PRINT TAB(2); "======================="
900 PRINT TAB(2); "TOTAL"
910 PRINT TAB(2); "STAKES"; TAB(9); "£"; J1
920 PRINT TAB(2); "TAX"; TAB(9); "£"; J7
930 PRINT TAB(2); "======================="
940 PRINT TAB(2); "TOTAL"
950 PRINT TAB(2); "OUTLAY"; TAB(9); "£"; K
960 PRINT TAB(2); "======================="
970 INPUT "PRESS RETURN TO CONTINUE"; V
971 CLS : PRINT ""
980 PRINT TAB(2); ODDSA; "/1"; TAB(7); "£"; H7; TAB(14); ODDSB; "/1";
    TAB(19); "£"; H8; TAB(26); ODDSC; "/1"; TAB(31); "£"; H9; TAB(38);
    ODDSD; "/1"; TAB(43); "£"; H10; TAB(49); "£"; J7; TAB(56); "£"; K
990 PRINT TAB(7); "("; J3; ")"; TAB(19); "("; J4; ")"; TAB(31); "("; J5; ")";
    TAB(43); "("; J6; ")"
1000 FOR I = 1 TO Z
1010 ODDSD = ODDSD + 5
1020 REM
1030 T = .1
1040 H = ((ODDSA * ODDSB) - 1)
1050 H1 = ((ODDSA + ODDSB) + 2)
1060 H2 = H / H1
1070 O1 = H2
1080 H3 = ((ODDSD + ODDSD) - 1)
1090 H4 = ((ODDSC + ODDSD) + 2)
1100 H5 = H3 / H4
1110 O2 = H5
```

```
1120 S = ((P1) * (O2 - T)) + ((P2) * (1.1))
1130 S1 = ((O1 - T) * (O2 - T)) - 1.21
1140 S2 = S / S1
1150 S3 = ((P2) * (O1 - T)) + ((P1) * (1.1))
1160 S4 = ((O2 - T) * (O1 - T)) - 1.21
1170 S5 = S3 / S4
1180 S6 = S2 + S5
1190 H6 = S6 / 10
1200 R1 = ((O1) + (1)) * S2
1210 R2 = ((O2) + 1) * S5
1220 H17 = ((ODDSB + 1) * (S2)) / ((ODDSA + ODDSB) + (2))
1230 H7 = INT(H17 * 100 + .5) / 100 + .01
1240 H11 = INT(H7 * 100 + .5) / 100
1250 H18 = ((ODDSA + 1) * (S2)) / ((ODDSA + ODDSB) + (2))
1260 H8 = INT(H18 * 100 + .5) / 100 + .01
1270 H12 = INT(H8 * 100 + .5) / 100
1280 H19 = ((ODDSD + 1) * (S5)) / ((ODDSC + ODDSD) + (2))
1290 H9 = INT(H19 * 100 + .5) / 100 + .01
1300 H13 = INT(H9 * 100 + .5) / 100
1310 H21 = ((ODDSC + 1) * (S5)) / ((ODDSC + ODDSD) + (2))
1320 H10 = INT(H21 * 100 + .5) / 100 + .01
1330 H14 = INT(H10 * 100 + .5) / 100
1340 H15 = H11 + H12 + H13 + H14
1350 H16 = H15 / 10
1360 J15 = INT(H16 * 100 + .5) / 100
1370 J16 = INT(H16 * 100 + .5) / 100
1380 H17 = H15 + H16
1390 E1 = INT(H17 * 100 + .5) / 100
1400 J1 = H7 + H8 + H9 + H10
1410 E = INT(J1 * 100 + .5) / 100
1420 J2 = J1 / 10
1430 J33 = (ODDSA + 1) * H7
1440 J10 = INT(J3 * 100 + .5) / 100
1450 J44 = (ODDSB + 1) * H8: J4 = INT(J44 * 100 + .5) / 100
1460 J11 = INT(J4 * 100 + .5) / 100
1470 J55 = (ODDSC + 1) * H9: J5 = INT(J55 * 100 + .5) / 100
1480 J12 = INT(J5 * 100 + .5) / 100
1490 J66 = (ODDSD + 1) * H10
1500 J13 = INT(J6 * 100 + .5) / 100
```

```
1510 J77 = J1 / 10: J7 = INT(J77 * 100 + .5) / 100
1520 K99 = J1 + J7: K = INT(K99 * 100 + .5) / 100
1530 K1 = J3 - K
1540 K2 = J4 - K
1550 K3 = J5 - K
1560 K4 = J6 - K
1570 PRINT TAB(2); ODDSA; "/1"; TAB(7); "£"; H7; TAB(14); ODDSB; "/1";
     TAB(19); "£"; H8; TAB(26); ODDSC; "/1"; TAB(31); "£"; H9; TAB(38);
     ODDSD; "/1"; TAB(43); "£"; H10; TAB(49); "£"; J7; TAB(56); "£"; K
1580 PRINT TAB(7); "("; J3; ")"; TAB(19); "("; J4; ")"; TAB(31); "("; J5; ")";
     TAB(43); "("; J6; ")"
1590 NEXT I
```

FOUR AGAINST THE FIELD

Runners	Odds	Stake	Return	Profit
A	16-1	£3.59	£61.03	£50.07
B	16-1	£3.59	£61.03	£50.07
C	25-1	£1.39	£36.14	£25.18
D	25-1	£1.39	£36.14	£25.18
	Stakes	£9.96		
	Tax	£0.99		
	Total outlay	£10.95		

Total outlay £10.95.
If Runner A wins, profit £50.07.
If Runner B wins, profit £50.07.
If Runner C wins, profit £25.18.
If Runner D wins, profit £25.18.

Computer Program 7

Save and Run as "5FIELD"

PROGRAMME 7 - 5FIELD

```
10 CLS : PRINT "'
30 INPUT "PROFIT TARGET £"; P1
40 REM
50 PRINT TAB(2); "FIVE AGAINST THE FIELD"
60 PRINT TAB(2); "(PROFIT TARGET....£"; P1; ")"
65 PRINT TAB(2); "============================="
70 PRINT
72 PRINT
130 INPUT "ODDS OF RUNNER A "; ODDSA
140 INPUT "ODDS OF RUNNER B "; ODDSB
150 INPUT "ODDS OF RUNNER C "; ODDSC
160 INPUT "ODDS OF RUNNER D "; ODDSD
170 INPUT "ODDS OF RUNNER E "; ODDSE
175 PRINT
180 PRINT
190 REM
200 PRINT
210 INPUT "NUMBER OF LINES "; Z
220 INPUT "PRESS RETURN TO CONTINUE"; Z
270 CLS : PRINT
272 REM
275 P1 = P1: P2 = P1
280 T = .1
290 R = (ODDSA * ODDSB) - 1
300 R1 = (ODDSA + ODDSB) + 2
310 R3 = R / R1
320 J = (ODDSD + 1) * (ODDSE + 1)
330 J1 = (ODDSC + 1) * (ODDSE + 1)
340 J2 = (ODDSC + 1) * (ODDSD + 1)
350 J3 = J + J1 + J2
360 J4 = (ODDSC + 1) * J
370 J5 = J4 - J3
380 J6 = J5 / J3
```

```
390 O1 = R3: O2 = J6: T = .1
400 S = ((P1) * (O2 - T)) + ((P2) * (1.1))
410 S1 = ((O1 - T) * (O2 - T)) - 1.21
420 S2 = S / S1
430 PRINT
440 S3 = ((P2) * (O1 - T)) + ((P1) * (1.1))
450 S4 = ((O2 - T) * (O1 - T)) - 1.21
460 S5 = S3 / S4
470 J7 = ((J) * (S5)) / J6
480 R6 = ((ODDSB + 1) * (S2)) / R1
490 W = ODDSB + 1
500 W1 = ODDSA + 1
510 W2 = W + W1
520 WW = (ODDSA + ODDSB) + 2
530 W24 = ((W) * (S2)) / W2
540 W4 = INT(W24 * 100 + .5) / 100 + .01
550 M = ((ODDSA + 1) * (W4))
560 W25 = ((W1) * (S2)) / W2
570 W5 = INT(W25 * 100 + .5) / 100 + .01
580 M1 = ((ODDSB + 1) * (W5))
590 T7 = W4 + W5
600 N = W / WW
610 N1 = N * R3
620 T18 = ((J) * (S5)) / J3
630 T8 = INT(T18 * 100 + .5) / 100 + .01
640 M2 = ((ODDSC + 1) * (T8))
650 T19 = ((J1) * (S5)) / J3
660 T9 = INT(T19 * 100 + .5) / 100 + .01
670 M3 = ((ODDSD + 1) * (T9))
680 T110 = ((J2) * (S5)) / J3
690 T10 = INT(T110 * 100 + .5) / 100 + .01
700 M4 = ((ODDSE + 1) * (T10))
710 T11 = W4 + W5 + T8 + T9 + T10
720 X = W5 + T8 + T9 + T10 + W4
730 X111 = X / 10: X1 = INT(X111 * 100 + .5) / 100
740 X2 = X + X1
750 Y = M - X2
760 Y1 = M1 - X2
770 Y2 = M2 - X2
```

```
780 Y3 = M3 - X2
790 Y4 = M4 - X2
810 PRINT TAB(2); "==========================="
820 PRINT TAB(2); "ODDS"; TAB(10); "STAKE"; TAB(17); "RETURN";
    TAB(26); "PROFIT"
830 PRINT TAB(2); "==========================="
840 PRINT TAB(2); "(A)"; ODDSA; "/1"; TAB(10); "£"; W4; TAB(17); "£"; M;
    TAB(26); "£"; Y
850 PRINT TAB(2); "(A)"; ODDSB; "/1"; TAB(10); "£"; W5; TAB(17); "£"; M1;
    TAB(26); "£"; Y1
860 PRINT TAB(2); "(A)"; ODDSC; "/1"; TAB(10); "£"; T8; TAB(17); "£"; M2;
    TAB(26); "£"; Y2
870 PRINT TAB(2); "(A)"; ODDSD; "/1"; TAB(10); "£"; T9; TAB(17); "£"; M3;
    TAB(26); "£"; Y3
880 PRINT TAB(2); "(A)"; ODDSE; "/1"; TAB(10); "£"; T10; TAB(17); "£"; M4;
    TAB(26); "£"; Y4
890 PRINT TAB(10); "=============="
900 PRINT TAB(2); "STAKES"; TAB(10); "£"; X
910 PRINT TAB(2); "TAX..."; TAB(10); "£"; X1
920 PRINT TAB(10); "=============="
930 PRINT TAB(2); "TOTAL"
940 PRINT TAB(2); "OUTLAY"; TAB(10); "£"; X2
950 PRINT TAB(10); "=============="
960 PRINT
970 PRINT TAB(2); "TOTAL OUTLAY (INC TAX PAID) £"; X2
982 PRINT TAB(2); "IF ANY ONE OF THE FIVE SELECTIONS"
984 PRINT TAB(2); "IS THE WINNER. NET PROFIT IS £"; P1
```

FIVE AGAINST THE FIELD
(Profit Target £50)

Runners	Odds	Stake	Return	Profit
A	10-1	£6.56	£72.16	£50.08
B	15-1	£4.51	£72.16	£50.08
C	20-1	£3.44	£72.24	£50.16
D	25-1	£2.78	£72.28	£50.20
E	25-1	£2.78	£72.28	£50.20
	Stakes	£20.07		
	Tax	£2.01		
	Total outlay	£22.08		

Total outlay (including tax) £22.08.
If any one of the five selections is the winner, net profit is £50.

Computer Program 8

Save and Run as "5(1+4)"

PROGRAMME 8 - 5(1+4)
```
60 PRINT TAB(2); "FIVE AGAINST THE FIELD"
70 PRINT TAB(2); "======================="
80 PRINT
150 INPUT "ODDS OF RUNNER A "; ODDSA
160 INPUT "ODDS OF RUNNER B "; ODDSB
170 INPUT "ODDS OF RUNNER C "; ODDSC
180 INPUT "ODDS OF RUNNER D "; ODDSD
190 INPUT "ODDS OF RUNNER E "; ODDSE
200 PRINT
210 INPUT "RUNNER A PROFIT.....£"; P1
220 INPUT "TEAM B/C/D/E PROFIT.£"; P2
280 J = ((ODDSC + 1) * (ODDSD + 1) * (ODDSE + 1))
290 J1 = ((ODDSB + 1) * (ODDSD + 1) * (ODDSE + 1))
300 J2 = ((ODDSB + 1) * (ODDSC + 1) * (ODDSE + 1))
310 J3 = ((ODDSB + 1) * (ODDSC + 1) * (ODDSD + 1))
320 J4 = J + J1 + J2 + J3
330 R = ((ODDSB + 1) * (J))
340 J5 = R - J4
350 J6 = J5 / J4
360 O1 = ODDSA: O2 = J6
370 T = .1
380 S = ((P1) * (O2 - T)) + ((P2) * (1.1))
390 S1 = ((O1 - T) * (O2 - T)) - 1.21
400 S2 = S / S1
410 S3 = ((P2) * (O1 - T)) + ((P1) * (1.1))
420 S4 = ((O2 - T) * (O1 - T)) - 1.21
430 S5 = S3 / S4
440 T2 = S2 + S5
450 T3 = T2 / 10
460 T4 = T2 + T3
470 K = ((J) * (S5)) / J4
480 K1 = ((J1) * (S5)) / J4
```

```
490 K2 = ((J2) * (S5)) / J4
500 K3 = ((J3) * (S5)) / J4
510 K4 = S2 + K + K1 + K2 + K3
520 K5 = K4 / 10
530 K6 = K4 + K5
540 R = (ODDSA + 1) * S2
550 R1 = (ODDSB + 1) * K
560 R2 = (ODDSC + 1) * K1
570 R3 = (ODDSD + 1) * K2
580 R4 = (ODDSE + 1) * K3
590 S42 = S / S1
600 S2 = INT(S42 * 100 + .5) / 100 + .01
610 R44 = (ODDSA + 1) * S2
620 K45 = ((J) * (S5)) / J4
630 K = INT(K45 * 100 + .5) / 100 + .01
640 M = (ODDSB + 1) * K
650 K51 = ((J1) * (S5)) / J4
660 K = INT(K51 * 100 + .5) / 100 + .01
670 K1 = INT(K51 * 100 + .5) / 100 + .01
680 M1 = (ODDSC + 1) * K1
690 K32 = ((J2) * (S5)) / J4
700 K2 = INT(K32 * 100 + .5) / 100 + .01
710 M2 = (ODDSD + 1) * K2
720 K33 = ((J3) * (S5)) / J4
730 K3 = INT(K33 * 100 + .5) / 100 + .01
740 M3 = (ODDSE + 1) * K3
750 Y = S2 + K + K1 + K2 + K3
760 Y101 = Y / 10: Y1 = INT(Y101 * 100 + .5) / 100
770 Y2 = Y + Y1
780 Y33 = R44 - Y2: Y3 = INT(Y33 * 100 + .5) / 100
790 Y44 = M - Y2: Y4 = INT(Y44 * 100 + .5) / 100
800 Y55 = M1 - Y2: Y5 = INT(Y55 * 100 + .5) / 100
810 Y66 = M2 - Y2: Y6 = INT(Y66 * 100 + .5) / 100
820 Y77 = M3 - Y2: Y7 = INT(Y77 * 100 + .5) / 100
830 CLS : PRINT
832 REM
835 PRINT TAB(2); "FIVE AGAINST THE FIELD"
840 PRINT TAB(2); "======================="
```

```
850 PRINT TAB(2); "ODDS"; TAB(10); "STAKE"; TAB(18); "RETURN";
    TAB(26); "PROFIT"
870 PRINT TAB(2); "A"; ODDSA; "/1"; TAB(10); "£"; S2; TAB(18); "£"; R44;
    TAB(26); "£"; Y3
880 PRINT TAB(2); "B"; ODDSB; "/1"; TAB(10); "£"; K; TAB(18); "£"; M;
    TAB(26); "£"; Y4
890 PRINT TAB(2); "C"; ODDSC; "/1"; TAB(10); "£"; K1; TAB(18); "£"; M1;
    TAB(26); "£"; Y5
900 PRINT TAB(2); "D"; ODDSD; "/1"; TAB(10); "£"; K2; TAB(18); "£"; M2;
    TAB(26); "£"; Y6
910 PRINT TAB(2); "E"; ODDSE; "/1"; TAB(10); "£"; K3; TAB(18); "£"; M3;
    TAB(26); "£"; Y7
920 PRINT TAB(2); "======================"
930 PRINT TAB(2); "TOTAL"
940 PRINT TAB(2); "STAKES"; TAB(10); "£"; Y
950 PRINT TAB(2); "TAX..."; TAB(10); "£"; Y1
960 PRINT TAB(2); "======================"
970 PRINT TAB(2); "TOTAL"
980 PRINT TAB(2); "OUTLAY"; TAB(10); "£"; Y2
1000 PRINT
1010 PRINT TAB(2); "TOTAL OUTLAY (INC TAX) £"; Y2
1020 PRINT TAB(2); "IF RUNNER A WINS, PROFIT £"; P1
1030 PRINT TAB(2); "IF RUNNER B,C,D OR E"
1040 PRINT TAB(2); "WINS, PROFIT £"; P2
```

FIVE AGAINST THE FIELD

Runners	Odds	Stake	Return	Profit
A	10-1	£5.88	£64.68	£50.67
B	15-1	£1.90	£39.84	£25.83
C	20-1	£1.90	£39.90	£25.89
D	25-1	£1.53	£39.78	£25.77
E	25-1	£1.53	£39.78	£25.77
	Stakes	£12.74		
	Tax	£1.27		
	Total outlay	£14.01		

Total outlay (including tax) £14.01.
If Runner A wins, profit £50.
If Runner B, C, D or E wins profit £25.

Computer Program 9

Save and Run as "5(2+3)"

PROGRAMME 9 - 5(2+3)

```
10 CLS : PRINT
20 PRINT TAB(2); "FIVE AGAINST THE FIELD"
30 PRINT TAB(2); "==========================="
40 PRINT
50 INPUT "PROFIT TARGET TEAM A/B   £ "; P1
60 INPUT "PROFIT TARGET TEAM C/D/E £ "; P2
70 REM*** VDU 2,1,27,1,71,1,27,1,69
130 INPUT "ODDS OF RUNNER A "; ODDSA
140 INPUT "ODDS OF RUNNER B "; ODDSB
150 INPUT "ODDS OF RUNNER C "; ODDSC
160 INPUT "ODDS OF RUNNER D "; ODDSD
170 INPUT "ODDS OF RUNNER E "; ODDSE
180 PRINT
210 INPUT "NUMBER OF LINES "; Z
220 INPUT "PRESS RETURN TO CONTINUE"; V
270 CLS : PRINT
280 T = .1
290 R = (ODDSA * ODDSB) - 1
300 R1 = (ODDSA + ODDSB) + 2
310 R3 = R / R1
320 J = (ODDSD + 1) * (ODDSE + 1)
330 J1 = (ODDSC + 1) * (ODDSE + 1)
340 J2 = (ODDSC + 1) * (ODDSD + 1)
350 J3 = J + J1 + J2
360 J4 = (ODDSC + 1) * J
370 J5 = J4 - J3
380 J6 = J5 / J3
390 O1 = R3: O2 = J6: T = .1
400 S = ((P1) * (O2 - T)) + ((P2) * (1.1))
410 S1 = ((O1 - T) * (O2 - T)) - 1.21
420 S2 = S / S1
430 PRINT
440 S3 = ((P2) * (O1 - T)) + ((P1) * (1.1))
```

```
450 S4 = ((O2 - T) * (O1 - T)) - 1.21
460 S5 = S3 / S4
470 J7 = ((J) * (S5)) / J6
480 R6 = ((ODDSB + 1) * (S2)) / R1
490 W = (ODDSB + 1)
500 W1 = (ODDSA + 1)
510 W2 = W + W1
520 WW = (ODDSA + ODDSB) + 2
530 W24 = ((W) * (S2)) / W2
540 W4 = INT(W24 * 100 + .5) / 100 + .01
550 M = ((ODDSA + 1) * (W4))
560 W25 = ((W1) * (S2)) / W2
570 W5 = INT(W25 * 100 + .5) / 100 + .01
580 M1 = ((ODDSB + 1) * (W5))
590 T7 = (W4) + (W5)
600 N = W / WW
610 N1 = N * R3
620 T18 = ((J) * (S5)) / J3
630 T8 = INT(T18 * 100 + .5) / 100 + .01
640 M2 = ((ODDSC + 1) * (T8))
650 T19 = ((J1) * (S5)) / J3
660 T9 = INT(T19 * 100 + .5) / 100 + .01
670 M3 = ((ODDSD + 1) * (T9))
680 T110 = ((J2) * (S5)) / J3
690 T10 = INT(T110 * 100 + .5) / 100 + .01
700 M4 = ((ODDSE + 1) * (T10))
710 T11 = W4 + W5 + T8 + T9 + T10
720 X = W5 + T8 + T9 + T10 + W4
730 X111 = X / 10: X1 = INT(X111 * 100 + .5) / 100
740 X2 = X + X1
750 Y = M - X2
760 Y1 = M1 - X2
770 Y2 = M2 - X2
780 Y3 = M3 - X2
790 Y4 = M4 - X2
800 REM
810 REM
820 PRINT TAB(2); "ODDS"; TAB(9); "STAKE"; TAB(17); "RETURN"; TAB
    "PROFIT"
```

```
840 PRINT TAB(2); "A"; ODDSA; "/1"; TAB(10); "£"; W4; TAB(17); "£"; M;
     TAB(26); "£"; Y
850 PRINT TAB(2); "B"; ODDSB; "/1"; TAB(10); "£"; W5; TAB(17); "£"; M1;
     TAB(26); "£"; Y1
860 PRINT TAB(2); "C"; ODDSC; "/1"; TAB(10); "£"; T8; TAB(17); "£"; M2;
     TAB(26); "£"; Y2
870 PRINT TAB(2); "D"; ODDSD; "/1"; TAB(10); "£"; T9; TAB(17); "£"; M3;
     TAB(26); "£"; Y3
880 PRINT TAB(2); "E"; ODDSE; "/1"; TAB(10); "£"; T10; TAB(17); "£"; M4;
     TAB(26); "£"; Y4
890 PRINT TAB(2); "================================="
900 PRINT TAB(2); "STAKES"; TAB(10); "£"; X
910 PRINT TAB(2); "TAX"; TAB(10); "£"; X1
920 PRINT TAB(2); "================================="
930 PRINT TAB(2); "TOTAL"
940 PRINT TAB(2); "OUTLAY"; TAB(10); "£"; X2
960 PRINT
970 PRINT TAB(2); "TOTAL OUTLAY (INC TAX PAID) £"; X2
980 PRINT TAB(2); "IF EITHER RUNNER A OR RUNNER B IS"
990 PRINT TAB(2); "THE WINNER.. NET PROFIT £"; P1
999 PRINT
1000 PRINT TAB(2); "BUT IF C, D OR E IS THE WINNER"
1010 PRINT TAB(2); "NET PROFIT £"; P2
1030 PRINT
1040 INPUT "PRESS RETURN TO CONTINUE "; V
1045 REM
1050 PRINT TAB(2); ODDSA; "/1"; TAB(7); "£"; W4; TAB(14); ODDSB; "/1";
     TAB(19); "£"; W5; TAB(25); ODDSC; "/1"; TAB(30); "£"; T8; TAB(36);
     ODDSD; "/1"; TAB(42); "£"; T9; TAB(48); ODDSE; "/1"; TAB(53); "£";
     T10; TAB(59); "£"; X2
1060 REM
1070 FOR I = 1 TO Z
1080 T = .1
1090 ODDSE = ODDSE + 5
1100 R = (ODDSA * ODDSB) - 1
1110 R1 = (ODDSA + ODDSB) + 2
1120 R3 = R / R1
1130 J = (ODDSD + 1) * (ODDSE + 1)
1140 J1 = (ODDSC + 1) * (ODDSE + 1)
```

```
1150 J2 = (ODDSC + 1) * (ODDSD + 1)
1160 J3 = J + J1 + J2
1170 J4 = (ODDSC + 1) * J
1180 J5 = J4 - J3
1190 J6 = J5 / J3
1200 O1 = R3: O2 = J6: T = .1
1210 S = ((P1) * (O2 - T)) + ((P2) * (1.1))
1220 S1 = ((O1 - T) * (O2 - T)) - 1.21
1230 S2 = S / S1
1240 S3 = ((P2) * (O1 - T)) + ((P1) * (1.1))
1250 S4 = ((O2 - T) * (O1 - T)) - 1.21
1260 S5 = S3 / S4
1270 J7 = ((J) * (S5)) / J6
1280 R6 = ((ODDSB + 1) * (S2)) / R1
1290 W = ODDSB + 1
1300 W1 = ODDSA + 1
1310 W2 = W + W1
1320 WW = (ODDSA + ODDSB) + 2
1330 W24 = ((W) * (S2)) / W2
1340 W4 = INT(W24 * 100 + .5) / 100 + .01
1350 M = ((ODDSA + 1) * (W4))
1360 W25 = ((W1) * (S2)) / W2
1370 W5 = INT(W25 * 100 + .5) / 100 + .01
1380 M1 = ((ODDSB + 1) * (W5))
1390 T7 = (W4) + (W5)
1400 N = W / WW
1410 N1 = N * R3
1420 T18 = ((J) * (S5)) / J3
1430 T8 = INT(T18 * 100 + .5) / 100 + .01
1440 M2 = ((ODDSC + 1) * (T8))
1450 T19 = ((J1) * (S5)) / J3
1460 T9 = INT(T19 * 100 + .5) / 100 + .01
1470 M3 = ((ODDSD + 1) * (T9))
1480 T110 = ((J2) * (S5)) / J3
1490 T10 = INT(T110 * 100 + .5) / 100 + .01
1500 M4 = ((ODDSE + 1) * (T10))
1510 T11 = W4 + W5 + T8 + T9 + T10
1520 X = W5 + T8 + T9 + T10 + W4
1530 X111 = X / 10: X1 = INT(X111 * 100 + .5) / 100
```

```
1540 X2 = X + X1
1550 Y = M - X2
1560 Y1 = M1 - X2
1570 Y2 = M2 - X2
1580 Y3 = M3 - X2
1590 Y4 = M4 - X2
1600 PRINT TAB(2); ODDSA; "/1"; TAB(7); "£"; W4; TAB(14); ODDSB; "/1";
     TAB(19); "£"; W5; TAB(25); ODDSC; "/1"; TAB(30); "£"; T8; TAB(36);
     ODDSD; "/1"; TAB(42); "£"; T9; TAB(48); ODDSE; "/1"; TAB(53); "£";
     T10; TAB(59); "£"; X2
1610 NEXT I
```

FIVE AGAINST THE FIELD

Runners	Odds	Stake	Return	Profit
A	10-1	£4.93	£54.23	£40.01
B	15-1	£3.40	£54.40	£40.18
C	20-1	£1.64	£34.44	£20.22
D	20-1	£1.64	£34.44	£20.22
E	25-1	£1.32	£34.32	£20.10
	Stakes	£12.93		
	Tax	£1.29		
	Total outlay	£14.22		

Total outlay (including tax) £14.22.
If either Runner A or Runner B is the winner, net profit £40.
But if C, D or E is the winner, net profit £20.

Computer Program 10
Save and Run as "6FIELD"

PROGRAMME 10 - 6FIELD

```
5 PRINT "SIX AGAINST THE FIELD"
7 PRINT "(SAME AMOUNT OF PROFIT FROM"
8 PRINT "WHICHEVER ONE WINS)"
10 CLS
20 PRINT ""
30 INPUT "ODDS OF RUNNER A "; ODDSA
40 INPUT "ODDS OF RUNNER B "; ODDSB
50 INPUT "ODDS OF RUNNER C "; ODDSC
60 INPUT "ODDS OF RUNNER D "; ODDSD
70 INPUT "ODDS OF RUNNER E "; ODDSE
80 INPUT "ODDS OF RUNNER F "; ODDSF
90 PRINT '
100 INPUT "PROFIT TARGET £"; P1
120 PRINT ""
130 INPUT "PRESS RETURN TO CONTINUE.."; V
140 CLS
150 PRINT "
155 P2 = P1
160 N = (ODDSB + 1) * (ODDSC + 1)
170 N1 = (ODDSA + 1) * (ODDSC + 1)
180 N2 = (ODDSA + 1) * (ODDSB + 1)
190 N3 = N + N1 + N2
200 N4 = (ODDSA + 1) * N
210 N5 = N4 - N3
220 N6 = N5 / N3
230 L = (ODDSE + 1) * (ODDSF + 1)
240 L1 = (ODDSD + 1) * (ODDSF + 1)
250 L2 = (ODDSD + 1) * (ODDSE + 1)
260 L3 = L + L1 + L2
270 L4 = (ODDSD + 1) * L
280 L5 = L4 - L3
290 L6 = L5 / L3
300 O1 = N6
310 O2 = L6
320 T = .1
```

```
330 S = ((P1 * (O2 - T))) + (P2) * (1.1)
340 S1 = ((O1 - T) * (O2 - T)) - 1.21
350 S2 = S / S1
360 S3 = ((P2) * (O1 - T)) + ((P1) * (1.1))
370 S4 = ((O2 - T) * (O1 - T)) - 1.21
380 S5 = S3 / S4
390 T2 = S2 + S5
400 T3 = T2 / 10
410 T4 = T2 + T3
420 R = (N / N3) * S2
430 R1 = (N1 / N3) * S2
440 R2 = (N2 / N3) * S2
450 R3 = (L / L3) * S5
460 R4 = (L1 / L3) * S5
470 R5 = (L2 / L3) * S5
480 T8 = R + R1 + R2 + R3 + R4 + R5
490 T9 = T8 / 10
500 T10 = T8 / T9
560 K15 = (ODDSA + 1) * R
570 K = INT(K15 * 100 + .5) / 100 + .01
950 PRINT
960 Z = INT(R * 100 + .5) / 100 + .01
970 Z1 = INT(R1 * 100 + .5) / 100 + .01
980 Z2 = INT(R2 * 100 + .5) / 100 + .01
990 Z3 = INT(R3 * 100 + .5) / 100 + .01
1000 Z4 = INT(R4 * 100 + .5) / 100 + .01
1010 Z5 = INT(R5 * 100 + .5) / 100 + .01
1020 Z6 = Z + Z1 + Z2 + Z3 + Z4 + Z5
1030 Z77 = (Z6) * (10) / 100
1032 Z7 = INT(Z77 * 100 + .5) / 100
1040 Z8 = Z6 + Z7
1050 N = (ODDSA + 1) * Z
1060 N1 = INT(N * 100 + .5) / 100 + .01
1070 N = (ODDSA + 1) * Z
1080 N1 = INT(Z * 100 + .5) / 100 + .02
1090 L = (ODDSA + 1) * Z
1100 N1 = (ODDSB + 1) * Z1
1110 N2 = (ODDSC + 1) * Z2
1120 N3 = (ODDSD + 1) * Z3
```

```
1130 N4 = (ODDSE + 1) * Z4
1140 N5 = (ODDSF + 1) * Z5
1150 PRINT "
1170 CLS : PRINT "
1180 REM
1190 PRINT TAB(9); "SIX AGAINST THE FIELD"
1192 PRINT TAB(9); "(PROFIT TARGET £"; P1; ")"
1200 PRINT TAB(9); "============================="
1210 PRINT TAB(2); "ODDS"; TAB(10); "STAKE"; TAB(19); "RETURN";
     TAB(29); "PROFIT"
1230 V1 = L - Z8
1240 V2 = INT(V1 * 100 + .5) / 100
1250 V3 = N1 - Z8
1260 V4 = INT(V3 * 100 + .5) / 100
1270 V5 = N2 - Z8
1280 V6 = INT(V5 * 100 + .5) / 100
1290 V7 = N3 - Z8
1300 V8 = INT(V7 * 100 + .5) / 100
1310 V9 = N4 - Z8
1320 V10 = INT(V9 * 100 + .5) / 100
1322 V11 = N5 - Z8
1324 V12 = INT(V11 * 100 + .5) / 100
1330 PRINT TAB(2); "A"; ODDSA; "/1"; TAB(10); "£"; Z; TAB(19); "£"; L;
     TAB(29); "£"; V2
1340 PRINT TAB(2); "B"; ODDSB; "/1"; TAB(10); "£"; Z1; TAB(19); "£"; N1;
     TAB(29); "£"; V4
1350 PRINT TAB(2); "C"; ODDSC; "/1"; TAB(10); "£"; Z2; TAB(19); "£"; N2;
     TAB(29); "£"; V6
1360 PRINT TAB(2); "D"; ODDSD; "/1"; TAB(10); "£"; Z3; TAB(19); "£"; N3;
     TAB(29); "£"; V8
1370 PRINT TAB(2); "E"; ODDSE; "/1"; TAB(10); "£"; Z4; TAB(19); "£"; N4;
     TAB(29); "£"; V10
1380 PRINT TAB(2); "F"; ODDSF; "/1"; TAB(10); "£"; Z5; TAB(19); "£"; N5;
     TAB(29); "£"; V12
1390 PRINT TAB(2); "============================"
1400 PRINT TAB(2); "TOTAL"
1410 PRINT TAB(2); "STAKES"; TAB(10); "£"; Z6
1420 PRINT TAB(2); "TAX"; TAB(10); "£"; Z7
1430 PRINT TAB(2); "============================"
```

```
1440 PRINT TAB(2); "TOTAL"
1450 PRINT TAB(2); "OUTLAY"; TAB(10); "£"; Z8
1470 PRINT
1480 PRINT TAB(2); "TOTAL OUTLAY £"; Z8
1482 PRINT TAB(2); "(INCLUDING TAX)"
1485 PRINT
1490 PRINT TAB(2); "IF ANY ONE OF THE 6 SELECTIONS"
1500 PRINT TAB(2); "IS THE WINNER..NET PROFIT £"; P1
```

SIX AGAINST THE FIELD
(Profit Target £50)

Runners	Odds	Stake	Return	Profit
A	10-1	£7.09	£77.99	£50.02
B	15-1	£4.88	£78.08	£50.11
C	20-1	£3.72	£78.12	£50.15
D	20-1	£3.72	£78.12	£50.15
E	25-1	£3.01	£78.26	£50.29
F	25-1	£3.01	£78.26	£50.29
Stakes		£25.43		
Tax		£2.54		
Total outlay		£27.97		

Total outlay (including tax paid on) £27.97.
If any one of the six selections is the winner, net profit
£50.

Your
Staking
Tables

Two Against The Field
— PROFIT TARGET —
£   .00

Odds	Stake	Odds	Stake	Total Outlay
-1	£ .	Evens	£ .	£ .
-1	£ .	13-8	£ .	£ .
-1	£ .	2-1	£ .	£ .
-1	£ .	9-4	£ .	£ .
-1	£ .	3-1	£ .	£ .
-1	£ .	7-2	£ .	£ .
-1	£ .	4-1	£ .	£ .
-1	£ .	9-4	£ .	£ .
-1	£ .	5-1	£ .	£ .
-1	£ .	11-2	£ .	£ .
-1	£ .	6-1	£ .	£ .
-1	£ .	13-2	£ .	£ .
-1	£ .	7-1	£ .	£ .
-1	£ .	15-2	£ .	£ .
-1	£ .	8-1	£ .	£ .
-1	£ .	9-1	£ .	£ .
-1	£ .	10-1	£ .	£ .

Three Against The Field
— PROFIT TARGET —
£   .00

Odds	Stake	Odds	Stake	Odds	Stake	Tax	Outlay
-1	£ .	Evens	£ .	-1	£ .	.	£ .
-1	£ .	13-8	£ .	-1	£ .	.	£ .
-1	£ .	2-1	£ .	-1	£ .	.	£ .
-1	£ .	9-4	£ .	-1	£ .	.	£ .
-1	£ .	3-1	£ .	-1	£ .	.	£ .
-1	£ .	7-2	£ .	-1	£ .	.	£ .
-1	£ .	4-1	£ .	-1	£ .	.	£ .
-1	£ .	9-2	£ .	-1	£ .	.	£ .
-1	£ .	5-1	£ .	-1	£ .	.	£ .
-1	£ .	11-2	£ .	-1	£ .	.	£ .
-1	£ .	6-1	£ .	-1	£ .	.	£ .
-1	£ .	13-2	£ .	-1	£ .	.	£ .
-1	£ .	7-1	£ .	-1	£ .	.	£ .
-1	£ .	15-2	£ .	-1	£ .	.	£ .
-1	£ .	8-1	£ .	-1	£ .	.	£ .
-1	£ .	17-2	£ .	-1	£ .	.	£ .
-1	£ .	9-1	£ .	-1	£ .	.	£ .
-1	£ .	10-1	£ .	-1	£ .	.	£ .

Four Against The Field
— PROFIT TARGET —
£   .00

Odds	Stake	Odds	Stake	Odds	Stake	Odds	Stake	Total
-1	£ .	Evens	£ .	-1	£ .	-1	£ .	£ .
-1	£ .	13-8	£ .	-1	£ .	-1	£ .	£ .
-1	£ .	2-1	£ .	-1	£ .	-1	£ .	£ .
-1	£ .	9-4	£ .	-1	£ .	-1	£ .	£ .
-1	£ .	3-1	£ .	-1	£ .	-1	£ .	£ .
-1	£ .	7-2	£ .	-1	£ .	-1	£ .	£ .
-1	£ .	4-1	£ .	-1	£ .	-1	£ .	£ .
-1	£ .	9-2	£ .	-1	£ .	-1	£ .	£ .
-1	£ .	5-1	£ .	-1	£ .	-1	£ .	£ .
-1	£ .	11-2	£ .	-1	£ .	-1	£ .	£ .
-1	£ .	6-1	£ .	-1	£ .	-1	£ .	£ .
-1	£ .	13-2	£ .	-1	£ .	-1	£ .	£ .
-1	£ .	7-1	£ .	-1	£ .	-1	£ .	£ .
-1	£ .	15-2	£ .	-1	£ .	-1	£ .	£ .
-1	£ .	8-1	£ .	-1	£ .	-1	£ .	£ .
-1	£ .	17-2	£ .	-1	£ .	-1	£ .	£ .
-1	£ .	9-1	£ .	-1	£ .	-1	£ .	£ .
-1	£ .	10-1	£ .	-1	£ .	-1	£ .	£ .

Five Against The Field
— PROFIT TARGET —
£   .00

Odds	Stake	Odds	Stake	Odds	Stake	Odds	Stake	Odds	Stake	Total
-1	£ .	Evens	£ .	-1	£ .	-1	£ .	-1	£ .	£ .
-1	£ .	13-8	£ .	-1	£ .	-1	£ .	-1	£ .	£ .
-1	£ .	2-1	£ .	-1	£ .	-1	£ .	-1	£ .	£ .
-1	£ .	9-4	£ .	-1	£ .	-1	£ .	-1	£ .	£ .
-1	£ .	3-1	£ .	-1	£ .	-1	£ .	-1	£ .	£ .
-1	£ .	7-2	£ .	-1	£ .	-1	£ .	-1	£ .	£ .
-1	£ .	4-1	£ .	-1	£ .	-1	£ .	-1	£ .	£ .
-1	£ .	9-2	£ .	-1	£ .	-1	£ .	-1	£ .	£ .
-1	£ .	5-1	£ .	-1	£ .	-1	£ .	-1	£ .	£ .
-1	£ .	11-2	£ .	-1	£ .	-1	£ .	-1	£ .	£ .
-1	£ .	6-1	£ .	-1	£ .	-1	£ .	-1	£ .	£ .
-1	£ .	13-2	£ .	-1	£ .	-1	£ .	-1	£ .	£ .
-1	£ .	7-1	£ .	-1	£ .	-1	£ .	-1	£ .	£ .
-1	£ .	15-2	£ .	-1	£ .	-1	£ .	-1	£ .	£ .
-1	£ .	8-1	£ .	-1	£ .	-1	£ .	-1	£ .	£ .
-1	£ .	17-2	£ .	-1	£ .	-1	£ .	-1	£ .	£ .
-1	£ .	9-1	£ .	-1	£ .	-1	£ .	-1	£ .	£ .
-1	£ .	10-1	£ .	-1	£ .	-1	£ .	-1	£ .	£ .

Six Against The Field
— PROFIT TARGET —
£   .00

Odds	Stake	Odds	Stake	Odds	Stake	Odds	Stake	Odds	Stake	Odds	Stake	Total
-1	£	Evens	£	-1	£	-1	£	-1	£	-1	£	£
-1	£	13-8	£	-1	£	-1	£	-1	£	-1	£	£
-1	£	2-1	£	-1	£	-1	£	-1	£	-1	£	£
-1	£	9-4	£	-1	£	-1	£	-1	£	-1	£	£
-1	£	3-1	£	-1	£	-1	£	-1	£	-1	£	£
-1	£	7-2	£	-1	£	-1	£	-1	£	-1	£	£
-1	£	4-1	£	-1	£	-1	£	-1	£	-1	£	£
-1	£	9-2	£	-1	£	-1	£	-1	£	-1	£	£
-1	£	5-1	£	-1	£	-1	£	-1	£	-1	£	£
-1	£	11-2	£	-1	£	-1	£	-1	£	-1	£	£
-1	£	6-1	£	-1	£	-1	£	-1	£	-1	£	£
-1	£	13-2	£	-1	£	-1	£	-1	£	-1	£	£
-1	£	7-1	£	-1	£	-1	£	-1	£	-1	£	£
-1	£	15-2	£	-1	£	-1	£	-1	£	-1	£	£
-1	£	8-1	£	-1	£	-1	£	-1	£	-1	£	£
-1	£	17-2	£	-1	£	-1	£	-1	£	-1	£	£
-1	£	9-1	£	-1	£	-1	£	-1	£	-1	£	£
-1	£	10-1	£	-1	£	-1	£	-1	£	-1	£	£

Two Against The Field
— MAXIMUM OUTLAY —
£   .00

Odds	Stake		Odds	Stake		Returns			
-1	£	.	Evens	£	.	A£	.	B£	.
-1	£	.	13-8	£	.	A£	.	B£	.
-1	£	.	2-1	£	.	A£	.	B£	.
-1	£	.	9-4	£	.	A£	.	B£	.
-1	£	.	3-1	£	.	A£	.	B£	.
-1	£	.	7-2	£	.	A£	.	B£	.
-1	£	.	4-1	£	.	A£	.	B£	.
-1	£	.	9-4	£	.	A£	.	B£	.
-1	£	.	5-1	£	.	A£	.	B£	.
-1	£	.	11-2	£	.	A£	.	B£	.
-1	£	.	6-1	£	.	A£	.	B£	.
-1	£	.	13-2	£	.	A£	.	B£	.
-1	£	.	7-1	£	.	A£	.	B£	.
-1	£	.	15-2	£	.	A£	.	B£	.
-1	£	.	8-1	£	.	A£	.	B£	.
-1	£	.	9-1	£	.	A£	.	B£	.
-1	£	.	10-1	£	.	A£	.	B£	.

Three Against The Field
— MAXIMUM OUTLAY —
£   .00

Odds	Stake	Odds	Stake	Odds	Stake
-1	£ .	Evens	£ .	-1	£ .
-1	£ .	13-8	£ .	-1	£ .
-1	£ .	2-1	£ .	-1	£ .
-1	£ .	9-4	£ .	-1	£ .
-1	£ .	3-1	£ .	-1	£ .
-1	£ .	7-2	£ .	-1	£ .
-1	£ .	4-1	£ .	-1	£ .
-1	£ .	9-2	£ .	-1	£ .
-1	£ .	5-1	£ .	-1	£ .
-1	£ .	11-2	£ .	-1	£ .
-1	£ .	6-1	£ .	-1	£ .
-1	£ .	13-2	£ .	-1	£ .
-1	£ .	7-1	£ .	-1	£ .
-1	£ .	15-2	£ .	-1	£ .
-1	£ .	8-1	£ .	-1	£ .
-1	£ .	17-2	£ .	-1	£ .
-1	£ .	9-1	£ .	-1	£ .
-1	£ .	10-1	£ .	-1	£ .